I greatly welcome this book. On reading it I felt a need fulfilled. Just what were those early studies like? Is it really true that in their vast scope and care for detail they have never been matched? (The answer is yes, it is true.) What are the advantages, disadvantages and pitfalls with various ways of quantifying data across a sample? Do we need statistics, and if so what sort? I found answers to these questions here.

PROFESSOR PAUL KERSWILL,
LANCASTER UNIVERSITY, UK

The ways in which data is collected, coded and analyzed provide the basis for trusting the conclusions reached in any sociolinguistic study. This detailed textbook critically examines methods used in quantitative sociolinguistic studies, including the ways in which the categories of age, gender, ethnicity and social class have been employed to chart language variation.

Quantitative Methods in Sociolinguistics

* *discusses the nature of data and explores methods of collecting evidence of language variation;
* *critically reviews the methodology in a number of sociolinguistic studies, showing the ways in which data has been collected and analyzed;
* *illustrates different ways of tabulating the results of an investigation and examines different ways of analyzing the results.

Designed for students at all levels studying sociolinguistics, this invaluable book evaluates and explains the basis on which claims have been made and encourages the reader to view the existing sociolinguistics literature with a more critical eye.

Ronald K.S. Macaulay is Emeritus Professor of Linguistics at Pitzer College. He is the author of books including Language, Social Class and Education (1997), Talk that Counts (2005) and The Social Art (2006).

Quantitative Methods in Sociolinguistics

RONALD K. S. MACAULAY

© Ronald K. S. Macaulay 2009

First published 2009 by
PALGRAVE MACMILLAN

Palgrave Macmillan in the UK is an imprint of Macmillan Publishers Limited, registered in England, company number 785998, of Houndmills, Basingstoke, Hampshire RG21 6XS.

Palgrave Macmillan in the US is a division of St Martin's Press LLC, 175 Fifth Avenue, New York, NY 10010.

Palgrave Macmillan is the global academic imprint of the above companies and has companies and representatives throughout the world.

Palgrave® and Macmillan® are registered trademarks in the United States, the United Kingdom, Europe and other countries.

ISBN-13: 978–0–230–57917–0 hardback
ISBN-10: 0–230–57917–5 hardback
ISBN-13: 978–0–230–57918–7 paperback
ISBN-10: 0–230–57918–3 paperback

This book is printed on paper suitable for recycling and made from fully managed and sustained forest sources. Logging, pulping and manufacturing processes are expected to conform to the environmental regulations of the country of origin.

A catalogue record for this book is available from the British Library.

A catalog record for this book is available from the Library of Congress.

10   9   8   7   6   5   4   3   2   1
18 17 16 15 14 13 12 11 10 09

Printed and bound in China

Contents

List of Illustrations

Figures

Tables

Foreword

... as Macaulay has frequently reminded us ...
(Cheshire, 2007: 159)

The motivation for this book goes back to 1965, when on a wintry February day in Bangor, Wales, I came across Bill Labov's article on Martha's Vineyard (Labov, 1963) in the library of the linguistics department. What immediately bowled me over was Labov's discovery of a new method of investigating language use, and this event has had a profound impact on my life since then. I ordered a copy of his New York study (Labov, 1966) as soon as it was published, and I was lucky enough to sit in on Labov's lectures and seminar at the 1966 Linguistic Institute at UCLA. What interested me most in what I learned from Labov was the importance of collecting information in a systematic and consistent fashion. When I was a graduate student at UCLA Bill Bright gave me the opportunity to review Walt Wolfram's Detroit study (Wolfram, 1969) and accepted a review that stretched to ten pages (Macaulay, 1970). On re-reading it, I am rather ashamed to see the confidence with which I criticized what Wolfram and the whole Detroit Survey (Shuy, Wolfram, and Riley, 1968a) had done, but my motivation was based on the view that "Labov's methods, if properly used, provide what is probably the most promising approach to the study of language that has yet emerged in the history of linguistics" (Macaulay, 1970: 773). In subsequent reviews of Fasold (1972) and Trudgill (1974), I continued to concentrate on the methodology (Macaulay, 1974, 1976a) because I believed (and still believe) that the future of sociolinguistics depends upon getting the methodology right. Of course, when I carried out my own empirical work (Macaulay and Trevelyan, 1973; Macaulay, 1977) I found that it was more difficult than I had implied to maintain such high standards in actual practice. Nevertheless, thirty years later I feel just as strongly that we need to examine the ways in which sociolinguistic investigation has been carried out and perhaps establish some basic principles of methodology.

It shocked me some years ago to discover that Labov's *Social Stratification of English in New York City* (Labov, 1966) was never reviewed in *Language* or any other major linguistics journal. There was no John the Baptist figure, playing the role of R.B. Lees, whose review of *Syntactic Structures* (Lees, 1957) introduced the new messiah of theoretical linguistics, Noam Chomsky. Some years ago, I suggested to Bill Bright or Dell Hymes (I cannot remember which) that it would be a good idea to devote a whole issue of *Language in Society* to a review of Labov's work by a number of sociolinguists and remedy this omission, but there was no interest in the idea. It is obvious from the volumes of *Language* and other journals that the work of Chomsky and other theoretical linguists is constantly under scrutiny and evaluation. There seems to be less interest in this kind of concern among sociolinguists. The present work is an attempt to review a number of sociolinguistic investigations with respect to their methodology to see what can be learned from them, both what to imitate and what to avoid. This requires examining some of the methodology in greater detail than is usually the case in commenting on previous work.

It will be obvious throughout that this is a very personal work and I have made no attempt to disguise my biases. I also have not attempted to conceal the fact that I know some of those scholars whose works I review. Although quantitative sociolinguistics is based on numbers, the numbers refer to people, and the decisions on how to collect those numbers and analyze them are made by people, not by machines. Sociolinguists are interested in people and are themselves interesting people. There is no reason to discuss their work as if it were produced by automata. Nor am I an automaton and I am grateful to Paul Kerswill, Stephen Levey, and Lee Munroe for their helpful comments and encouragement. My thanks also to Kitty Van-Boxel and the team at Newgen Imaging Systems for seeing the book through the process of publication.

Preface

If linguistics is, as is often claimed, the scientific study of language, then it is reasonable to expect linguists to behave like other scientists. One group of linguists has adopted the model of theoretical physicists in providing algorithmic explanations for idealized mental data. The extent to which these efforts have been successful remains a matter of dispute, but this book is not concerned with that branch of linguistics. Other linguists have approached language as a phenomenon that can be described by means of empirical observations, and this work examines one such approach.

Except for those who believe that language can be studied only as a Platonic form glimpsed in a cave of abstraction, the greatest challenge for investigators is how to deal with the vast variety of forms and uses that constitute a language. Over the past fifty years a number of different approaches to the empirical study of language have emerged and developed their own methodologies. These include ethnography of communication (Hymes, 1974), interactional sociolinguistics (Gumperz, 1982), conversational analysis (Sacks, 1992), and variationist sociolinguistics (Labov, 1966). Common to all these approaches is the notion that all claims about language should be based on observation of actual language use. The invention of the portable tape recorder made the study of speech possible in ways that would have been difficult if not impossible in earlier times. The evolution of computers has made possible new forms of analysis. However, the mere possibility of audio recording and electronic processing does not provide an answer to all the problems in the study of speech. In order to present convincing empirical evidence of language variation, it is necessary to collect the data in a systematic way, but the notion of data is a more complex one than is often assumed (Coombs, 1964).

This book is about the approach that has come to be known as Variationist Sociolinguistics (sometimes also known as Labovian Sociolinguistics) following the example set by William Labov in his pioneering works on Martha's Vineyard (Labov, 1963) and New York (Labov, 1966). The focus of the present work is on methodology and its aim is to examine critically the way the sociolinguistic evidence has been collected and analyzed. As Coupland points out:

Variationist sociolinguistics is self-consciously bullish about its empirical discovery procedures. It is clearly an empiricist research tradition. Its epistemology—its research philosophy—is grounded in neutral observation, minimizing observer-effects, and objective analysis of data through precise and replicable quantitative procedures.

(Coupland, 2007: 24)

However, there may be a methodological skeleton in the sociolinguistic cupboard. As Bailey and Tillery suggest, in an article entitled "Some sources of divergent data in sociolinguistics," "[o]ver the last twenty years ... the concern for methodological rigor has lessened considerably" (2004: 11). They point out that "[m]any recent sociolinguistic studies ... provide few details about how their informants were selected or about the representativeness of their samples" (2004: 20) and they claim that "the results in sociolinguistic research are sometimes as much a consequence of the methodology used as of the behavior of the informants" (2004: 27).

Many published articles include only a brief account of how the data were collected, coded, and analyzed though it is this information that provides the basis for trusting the conclusions reached in the study. However, these accounts are often so brief that much important information is omitted. As Macafee remarks, "little of the experience of fieldwork finds its way into published accounts of research" (1994: 42). (Macafee herself is an exception to this as she gives a very explicit account of her fieldwork and the kinds of problems she encountered.) Tagliamonte (2006: 17) remarks that "fieldwork methods may be the best-kept secret of sociolinguistics."

Wolfram (1993) also comments on the lack of information in some published accounts:

My own research encounters and experience teaching students to conduct variation analysis has taught me that the presentation of elegant-appearing summaries of results found in published versions of variation studies are often far removed from the laboratory in which such analyses are conducted. In the process, some of the critical procedural and analytical decisions may be disregarded or camouflaged, making the analysis seem much cleaner than it actually is.

(Wolfram, 1993: 194)

Like Macafee, Wolfram gives a clear account of his research procedures.

It is not only a question of accountability, however. The past fifty years have seen a range of approaches to investigating variation in speech but there is seldom discussion in the sociolinguistic literature of the merits of different methodologies. In 1972, Dell Hymes proposed a model for communicative acts. It is perhaps one sign of the lack of interest in methodology that Hymes' model appears to have had little impact on quantitative sociolinguistics. At the time Hymes proposed his model the main stylistic factor that was often examined in quantitative studies was "attention to speech," following Labov's (1966) example, and later on emerged the notion of "audience design" (Bell, 1984). Despite the range of work that has been produced in the past fifty years, there has been less progress in looking at the complexity of variation in speech samples recorded for sociolinguistic variation (Macaulay, 1999, 2005a; Eckert and Rickford, 2001).

In particular, little attention has been paid to the various aspects of the speech event that Hymes outlined. It is impossible to know to what extent the results from many studies have been affected by uncontrolled aspects of the speech event. There are clear cases where, for example, the effect of an interviewer has been examined (Douglas-Cowie, 1978; Rickford and McNair-Knox, 1994; Bailey and Tillery, 2004; Schilling-Estes, 2004), but in most cases it is apparently assumed that the role of the interviewer is neutral. There also have been a few attempts to look at different aspects of style-shifting (see, for example, the papers in Eckert and Rickford, 2001) but it is not a question that is regularly addressed in reports of investigations.

Our understanding of language ought to grow through the cumulative effect of the results from a variety of studies. It is reassuring when the results from one study are confirmed by those from a subsequent study. However, it is sometimes the case that the results from one study are contradicted by those from another (Bailey and Tillery, 2004). Whether certain earlier results are confirmed or contradicted, it is essential that the process by which the results have been obtained should be as transparent as possible. Otherwise, the source of the agreement or disagreement may be obscured. As Tagliamonte (2006: 95) points out the choices made in analysis "must be transparent enough for comparison with earlier research as well as future replications."

In presenting the results of a particular investigation it is common to cite earlier work, but it is hazardous to compare claims about, for example, age, gender, social class, or ethnic factors in other studies, if there are critical differences in the way that evidence has been collected. Establishing some greater consensus on methodological procedures for sociolinguistic research would provide a more solid base for the future of the field.

One of the aims of the present work is to provide a kind of cumulative retrospective review of works that I believe have made important contributions to the field. The main emphasis is on methodology because this is the area in which we can learn from each other's achievements but also from their missteps. In re-reading many of the works in preparation for this volume I have been impressed by the range and variety of methods employed and I hope that by drawing attention to these pioneering works future sociolinguists will be able to make good use of their examples.

The plan for the book is to examine choice points in the planning of a sociolinguistic investigation, looking at the kind of decisions investigators have made and exploring some of the consequences of certain decisions. Chapter 1 examines the kinds of social categories that have been used in correlational studies of language variation. Chapter 2 discusses the nature of data. Chapter 3 explores different methods of collecting data. Chapter 4 illustrates ways of tabulating the results, while Chapter 5 examines methods of analysis, and how to interpret the results. Chapter 6 is devoted to a detailed examination of nineteen book-length studies. Chapter 7 presents the results of an unpublished study of discourse variation.

In the chapters that follow I will critically examine a number of studies, including my own, pointing out that the ways in which decisions are made may significantly affect the results. Inevitably, pointing out what has and has not been done smacks of evaluation, in preparation for awarding grades. That is not the purpose of this book. (I am all too aware of the weaknesses in my own work to risk grading others.) The intention is not to criticize investigators for the decisions they have taken but rather to provide a framework in which future projects can be planned as effectively as possible. As Bailey and Tillery conclude: "Disentangling the effects of our methods from the effects of social and linguistic factors with some certainty is perhaps the most important thing we can do to build on the solid foundation laid by first-generation sociolinguists" (2004: 28). Coupland points out:

> A concept of "good data" exists in variationist sociolinguistic surveying and it relates to criteria of naturalness, untaintedness and representativeness, as well as to the need to get excellent acoustic quality in audio-recording.
>
> (Coupland, 2007: 25)

It is my hope that exploring methodological questions will help to provide more 'good data' and prove beneficial for the future of variationist sociolinguistics. We are all chasing the shadows in Plato's cave, unlike our colleagues in theoretical linguistics, who have direct access to the ideal forms through intuition. If this book helps to shed a little more light in the cave, it will have accomplished its purpose.

1 Social Categories

As stated in the preface, this book is concerned with the approach that has come to be known as variationist sociolinguistics, emanating from the pioneering work of Labov (1963, 1966). Basic to this approach is the notion that some kinds of linguistic variation have social significance. As Labov put it in his New York study:

> There are of course many kinds of variation that fall outside the scope of linguistic analysis. Lisp, stammer, hiss and whistle seem to be correlated with biological or psychological idiosyncrasies. Variations in tempo, volume or pitch or such voice qualifiers as rasp or nasality are very often idiosyncratic. In general, linguistic behavior, and only variations which have social significance can be considered relevant to linguistic structure.
>
> (Labov 1966: 49)

Consequently, those working in the field of variationist sociolinguistics generally look for some social or extralinguistic factor that may help to identify features of speech characteristic of groups of speakers. One of the essential methodological questions in any sociolinguistic investigation has been deciding on which factor(s) to examine. Although all speakers belong to multiple speech communities, four factors have proved the most durable: age, gender, ethnicity, and social class. This chapter will review how these factors have been employed in a range of variationist studies. Although some of these studies are quite old, it is worthwhile looking back to their methodology because of what Bailey and Tillery (2004: 28) call "the concern with methods that in part motivated the first generation of sociolinguists." That concern makes much of the earlier work still relevant.

Age

In principle, the easiest social factor to determine is age since at any given time an individual is a certain age, though some people may be reluctant to say what it is. Where precise information is not available, classification into broad categories can usually be estimated on the basis of appearance (Chambers, 1995). It is therefore not surprising that age regularly appears as an extralinguistic variable in sociolinguistic studies (e.g. Labov, 1963, 1966, 2004; Wolfram, 1969; Fasold, 1972; Trudgill, 1974; Macaulay, 1977; Feagin, 1979; Milroy, 1980; Haeri, 1996; McCafferty, 2001).

However, as Eckert (1996) has pointed out, using age as an extralinguistic variable is not a simple matter. The obvious problem is that age is a continuous variable so that for purposes of correlation with linguistic features, speakers must be classified in age groups. Thus any use of age as an extralinguistic variable requires a decision about how such age groups are to be identified and justified. Even a simple classification into adults and children is complex, not only because the age at which one can be counted as an adult is itself problematic but also because neither category will be homogeneous.

If age is to be included as an extralinguistic factor, decisions have to be made at the very start of planning the project. These will include the age range of speakers to be included. At how early an age does it make sense to include children in an investigation into variation in the community? Conversely, is there an age at which it makes little sense to include elderly people? What is the purpose of including speakers from a wide range of ages? Will speakers be selected in order to represent a particular age cohort or will age simply be one of the pieces of demographic information collected from the speakers? If the former, on what basis will the speakers be chosen? If the latter, how will the speakers be grouped into cohorts? These two approaches can be illustrated with two examples.

In my investigation of Glasgow speech (Macaulay and Trevelyan, 1973; Macaulay, 1977) the original plan for the study included the following age categories in order to provide a cross-section of the population:

10-year-old children attending primary school
15-year-old children attending secondary school
University students and young adults not attending university
Parents of primary and secondary school children
People over fifty

(Macaulay and Trevelyan, 1973: 19)

Since this sample was only one of three categories of speakers to be interviewed (the others were teachers and employers), this range of speakers proved too ambitious a target for one interviewer to complete in a period of four months. Accordingly, it was decided to eliminate the categories of university students/young adults and those over the age of 50. In commenting on this decision, Macaulay and Trevelyan report that, in retrospect, it would have been worthwhile increasing the number of parents interviewed to compensate for this reduction, but "it is in the nature of hindsight that it comes too late to be useful" (1973: 228). This comment is one that many researchers will echo. One of the aims of this book is the hope that some of this kind of hindsight can be replaced by foresight.

The choice of 10-year-olds and 15-year-olds was not unmotivated. Since the transition to secondary school in Scotland took place at 11–12 years of age, choosing the 10-year-old cohort provided a sample of primary school children who were not yet poised to enter secondary school. The choice of 15-year-olds was to include the whole range of adolescents of this age, since some would be leaving school at the age of 16. Obviously, different choices could have been made, but the decision to interview these two age groups was made for specific reasons. The analysis showed that for four out of the five phonological variables, there were age differences, though these intersected with gender and social class differences.

Trudgill (1974) chose his sample of 50 adults by means of a quasi-random sample based on the local register of electors. To this he added 10 schoolchildren, giving the sample shown in Example 1.1.

Age	#	%
10–19	10	16
20–29	12	20
30–39	6	6
40–49	9	15
50–59	14	24
60–69	10	6
70+	3	5

Source: (Calculated from Trudgill, 1974: 28, figure1)

Trudgill does not explain his decision to group his speakers by decades and it might be argued that there would have been advantages in grouping his speakers by some notion of different generations. In practice, as far as the results presented in Trudgill (1974) are concerned, this would have made little difference, since the main age difference found was between the youngest group and the adults in their use of the (e) variable, that is, the vowel in words such as *bell, well*, and *healthy* (Trudgill 1974: 105). For the diphthong in words such as *right, ride*, and *rye* Trudgill also found that there was a difference between those over 40 and the younger speakers. In neither of these findings was the division into decades crucial. Labov (1966) also divides his speakers into decades but similarly does not explain the motivation for this classification. To draw attention to this methodological decision is not to imply that it was wrong for Trudgill and Labov to do it this way, but the question that arises is whether their results would have been different if they had chosen a different classification into age groups. That is a question that only the researchers themselves can answer unless they provide all the information on which to base a reclassification. It also illustrates the importance of being fully explicit in describing methodological decisions.

Other investigators have chosen deliberately distinct age groups. Feagin (1979) chose "teenagers and men and women over 65" (1979: 23) for her primary sample in order to examine the possibility of linguistic change in Anniston. Fasold (1972) selected three age groups: children (10–12), adolescents (13–19), and adults (21 or older). Milroy (1980) divided her speakers into two groups 18–25 and 40–55, without further comment. Guy, Horvath, Vonwiller, Daisley, and Rogers (1986) divided the Sydney sample into four age groups 11–14, 15–19, 20–39, and 40 plus. Bailey, Wikle, Tillery, and Sand (1991) compared changes in four age groups 95–62, 61–45, 44–30, and 29–18. Cornips (1998) split her sample into "young" (20–45) and "old" (over 60). Dubois and Horvath (1998) identified three age groups in their Cajun sample (19–39; 40–59: 60 and over). Tagliamonte (1998) divided her York sample into four generations, 20–30, 30–50, 50–70, and over 70. Fridland (1999) in her study in Memphis has three age groups (over 65, 36–48, and under 25). In Derby, Foulkes and Docherty (1999) selected a younger group of speakers (aged 14–27) and an older group (aged 45–67) and in Newcastle, Watt and Milroy (1999) chose a similar sample, though their youngest speakers were age 15. In Glasgow, Stuart-Smith (1999) recorded equal numbers of adolescents (age 13–14) and adults (age 40–60). Kerswill and Williams (2000) chose age groups of 4, 8, and 12 in order to test a theory about age grading. Smith (2001) in her Buckie study has three age groups (22–31, 50–60, and 80+). Gordon (2001) chose adolescents (16–18) and adults (39–51) "two plainly separated age groups, rather than from a broad range of ages, in order to examine more clearly the generational differences expected of a change in progress" (2001: 42). McCafferty's (2001: 26) informal sampling method produced two categories, teenagers (12–19) and adults (54–73). McNair (2005) chose three groups: older people, born before 1926 who grew up during the Depression; middle-aged adults "who grew up in the 1950s and became young adults in the 1960s"; and young speakers "who grew up in the 1980s" (McNair 2005: 8). Dannenberg (2002: 73) also had three age groups: old (60+); middle (30–59); and young (10–29), but does not comment on the decision to choose these three groups. Llamas (2006) has four age groups "old" (60–80), "middle" (32–45), "young adult" (19–22) and "adolescent" (16–17) but adds that "young adults and adolescents, being almost contiguous, can be taken as a combined group of 16 young speakers" (2006: 98). Wolfram and Thomas (2002: 111–121) treat age as a continuous variable and compare the speakers according to date of birth. There have also been studies where the sample consisted of a single age group. For example, Wolfram (1973), Cheshire (1982), Cheshire, Kerswill and Williams (1999), Eckert (1989, 2000), and Stenström, Andersen, and Hasund (2002) all collected examples of adolescent speech. Coupland, Coupland and Giles (1991) examined the speech of the elderly.

It is clear that there is no agreement on how to treat age as a variable. In some cases, the groupings are presumably a consequence of the sample, even where it is not a judgment sample with the categories defined in advance. For example, in Milroy's Belfast sample of speakers she may have recorded no speakers between the ages of 25 and 40, so that the division into two groups would have seemed obvious, and the resultant analysis certainly showed some statistically significant age differences with this grouping (Milroy 1980: 124–130). However, it is impossible to know to what extent the results were affected by the choice of these two age groups to represent their communities. The same comment applies even more to those who have grouped their speakers into decades or generations. Would the results have been significantly different if an alternative grouping had been chosen? Without access to the raw data, it is impossible to test this. None of which means that there is any reason to challenge the results, but it is obvious from the examples cited above that what it means to be classified as "young" or "old" may vary considerably. It also underlines a point that will be made later. If the raw data had been presented with the results for individuals listed, it would be possible for other investigators to test for different age groupings.

Age will always be a relevant factor even where it is not a central concern of the project, but it is clear from the examples given above that there is no general agreement on what constitutes an appropriate age group in a sociolinguistic study. It is undeniable that our form of speech changes with age from our earliest babblings to our senile mutterings but exactly what changes at what age requires careful investigation. As Eckert has pointed out:

> The age continuum is commonly divided into equal chunks with no particular attention to the relation between these chunks and the life stages that make age socially significant. Rather, when the full age span is considered in community studies, the age continuum is generally interpreted as representing continuous apparent time. At some point, the individual's progress through normative life stages (e.g., school, work, marriage, childrearing, retirement) might be considered rather than, or in addition to, chronological age.
>
> (Eckert, 1996: 156)

Hazen (2000) illustrates this approach to the role of age in language variation. In a study of identity and ethnicity in North Carolina, he divided his subject pool into three age groups relative to the integration of the public schools:

> Using integration as the basis for age categorization yields three groups: those speakers who went to segregated schools exclusively, those who were in school during the time of integration, and those who began school after integration (i.e., after 1970).
>
> (Hazen, 2000: 9)

It will not always be the case that there is an obvious rationale for establishing age groups but any sociolinguistic project should be as explicit as possible about the reasons for decisions to group the speakers on the basis of age. Milroy and Gordon 2003) sum up their discussion of age:

> Age by itself has no explanatory value; it is only when examined in the context of its social significance as something reflecting differences in life experiences that it becomes a useful analytical construct.
>
> (Milroy and Gordon, 2003: 39)

This comment applies equally well to the other extralinguistic factors discussed in this chapter.

Gender

In comparison to age, gender, seen as a division into male and female, rather than sexual orientation, is relatively simple. Most people are accustomed to declaring their sex/gender in response to many kinds of enquiry and thus this information is usually available to the investigator. Gender is also generally fairly easy to determine on external criteria, although there may be ambiguous cases. Again it is not surprising that gender is one of the factors frequently examined in sociolinguistic investigations (e.g. Fischer, 1958; Labov, 1966, 2004; Wolfram, 1969; Fasold, 1972; Trudgill, 1974; Macaulay, 1977; Feagin, 1979; Milroy, 1980; Cheshire, 1982; Coupland, 1988; Haeri, 1996; Eckert, 2000; McCafferty, 2001).

Gender presents in a very clear form a challenge that confronts the investigation of all of the four extralinguistic factors. Any speech event, as Hymes (1974) showed, is a complex interaction of many components. Central to the situation is the relationship of the participants. Many scholars have criticized some of the early reports on gender differences because they were based on interviews carried out by male interviewers (Cameron, 1985). This is a problem not only for gender differences but also for age, ethnic, and social class differences, but gender differences present the problem in a simple and obvious way. Graddol and Swann (1989) also point out that Labov's (1966) questionnaire and reading passages were more appropriate for male interviewees.

Interviews are not the only way in which to collect data (see Chapter 3) but the problem remains in any method. Since the interaction in all male groups, or all female groups, or mixed groups is likely to differ, there is no neutral or unmarked case. If the focus is on gender, then it may be possible to set up procedures where speakers are recorded in all three situations, but in many kinds of investigations this would not be practical. If the data are to be collected through interviews, it might be preferable for females to be interviewed by a female investigator and males by a male interviewer. This would avoid the possibility that the interaction would be affected by the kinds of differences claimed in the two-culture model of gender differences in language (Maltz and Borker 1982; Tannen 1990) but it does not follow that all bias would be eliminated since the male and female interviewers might differ importantly in their form of speech and thus affect the kind of speech produced by the interviewee.

The question of interviewer bias is relevant to all four social categories. Differences in age, gender, ethnicity, and social class between the speaker and interviewer always have the potentiality to influence the interaction. The surprising thing is that it sometimes seems to matter less than might have been expected (Cukor-Avila and Bailey 2001; Macaulay 1991a).

Eckert and McConnell-Ginet (1992) also draw attention to the question of variability within a category:

> Tomboys and goody-goodies, home-makers and career women, body builders and fashion models, secretaries and executives, basketball coaches and French teachers, professors and students, mothers and daughters – these are all categories of girls and women whose mutual differences are part of their construction of themselves and each other as gendered beings.
>
> (Eckert and McConnell-Ginet, 1992: 470)

Similar comments could be made about individuals in all four social categories but they are particularly relevant to gender because it is the one dichotomous category. Milroy (1980), Cheshire (1982), Eckert (1989, 2000), and Fought (2003) have shown how social connections intersect with gender in affecting language variation. Meyerhoff (1996) points out that speakers will present different aspects of themselves according to the social situation and this may affect how gender differences are manifested and perceived.

Although gender differences continue to be examined in the variationist paradigm (e.g. Macaulay, 2005a), most investigation into gender differences has been qualitative (e.g., Coates, 1996, 2003; Holmes, 2006) where the methodological challenges are different.

Ethnicity

Ethnicity is an even more problematic category than gender, not least because it can be used in reference to a number of characteristics: race, nationality, religion. For example, Labov (1966: 193) lists the distribution of his speakers by ethnic group: Negro (32), Jewish, Orth. (23), Jewish, Cons. and Ref. (24), Catholic (35), and Protestant (8). However, when he comes to examine the ethnic group as an independent variable, Labov (1966: 292) lists only three categories: Jews (45), Italians (19), and Negroes (9). He comments: "The balance of the population consists of eight informants of various backgrounds: two Ukrainians, and one each of Irish, German, Greek, Spanish, and Norwegian backgrounds. One informant came from a Negro background but is now a part of the white group for all practical purposes" (1966: 292). This reveals a shift from the original classification into racial and religious groups to a classification at least partly based on country of origin; the religious difference between Catholics and Protestants is no longer mentioned. Labov, in a footnote, quotes from Glazer and Moynihan (1963):

> The mere existence of a name itself is perhaps sufficient to form group character in new situations, for the name associates an individual, who can actually be anything, with a certain past, country, race. But as a matter of fact, someone who is Irish or Jewish or Italian generally has other traits than the mere existence of the name that associates him with other people attached to the group. A man is connected to his group by ties of family and friendship. But he is also connected by ties of *interest*. The ethnic groups in New York are also *interest groups*.
>
> (Glazer and Moynihan, 1963: 16–17)

Giles (1979) points out the difficulty of dealing with ethnicity as a social category because of "the thousands of distinct ethnic groups around the world which vary simultaneously on a vast range of dimensions, including history, territory, demography, institutional support and their economic and political relationships with other contrasting ethnic groups" (1979: 251). Giles, following Barth (1969),, opts for a notion of ethnicity that depends upon how individuals identify themselves. Wolfram (1973) gives a very careful analysis of the situation of Puerto Ricans in New York City, showing the complexity of the notion of ethnicity for a group that is identified by immigrant status, race, and social class.

In my investigation of Glasgow speech (Macaulay, 1977), I included religion as subsidiary variable, as forty percent of the population were identified as Catholic. Religion is linked to ethnicity because most of the Catholics are of Irish descent (Macafee, 1994: 13). Since there are state-run Catholic schools at all levels in Glasgow, it was possible that there would be marked differences in speech. For the five variables I examined, however, there were no significant differences that could be related to religion.

McCafferty (2001), in his study of (London) Derry in Northern Ireland, gives a very careful account of ethnicity, making clear that religion is an uncertain indicator of ethnicity:

> ...it is possible to have no religion whatsoever, but still regard oneself (perhaps unwillingly), and be regarded by others, as "Catholic" or "Protestant" in the ethnic sense.
>
> (McCafferty, 2001: 25)

As Azoulay (1997: 41) observes: "Identity is formed in the interstice between recognition and being recognized." This kind of recognition can have far-reaching consequences. In (London) Derry, where 70 percent of the population is Roman Catholic, McCafferty points out that the groups are not only segregated by where they live but also by what they do (or can do):

> But activity segregation is perhaps even more important than the residential kind: many activities are organised wholly within one community or the other, and amenities are frequently located in such a way that activity mixing is out of the question for many.
>
> (McCafferty, 2001: 211)

This observation is exemplified by the case of the Lumbee American Indians in North Carolina (Wolfram and Dannenberg, 1999; Dannenberg, 2002; Schilling-Estes, 2004). Although the Lumbee are the largest non-reservation group of Native Americans in the U.S., they have had difficulty in asserting their identity as a Native American tribe because they have no ancestral language. Yet the Lumbee constitute a distinct ethnic group.

Fought (2002), in her chapter on ethnicity in the *Handbook of Language Variation and Change*, compares ethnicity as a category to Eckert and

McConnell's (1992) view of gender:

> ... race as a category is useless to us without an understanding of the construction of ethnicity by individuals and communities. As has been shown for gender, ethnicity is not about what one *is*, but rather about what one *does*.
>
> (Fought, 2002: 444)

Labov's example about the informant "from a Negro background" who was then "part of the white group *for all practical purposes*" (Labov, 1966: 292, emphasis added) can be seen as illustrating Fought's point.

Any sociolinguistic investigation that includes ethnicity as an extralinguistic category needs to specify very clearly how membership in that category is established. However, in many investigations the target population is not ethnically diverse and thus such differences will not be salient in the community.

Social class

Social class is a category that has received regular attention from the earliest sociolinguistic studies (e.g. Fischer, 1958; Labov, 1966; Wolfram, 1969; Fasold, 1972; Trudgill, 1974; Macaulay, 1977; Feagin, 1979) and has continued to be examined in later studies (e.g. Coupland, 1988; Macaulay, 1991a; Haeri, 1996; Labov, 2001; McCafferty, 2001; Macaulay, 2005a), though it has received less consistent attention than in the earlier studies. However, social class is a much more problematic category than the other three. In some studies (e.g. Labov, 1966; Trudgill, 1974), social class is treated as a continuous variable, similar to age, so that some criteria must be adopted for assigning speakers to a particular category. In other studies (e.g. Macaulay, 1991a, 2005a; Stuart-Smith, 1999; Cheshire, Kerswill and Williams, 1999) social class is treated as a dichotomous variable, similar in this respect to gender.

Despite receiving considerable attention in recent years by a range of scholars (e.g., see the references in Crompton, Devine, Savage, and Scott, 2000), social class remains a controversial subject with many conflicting views. From Lloyd Warner's pioneering studies (Warner, Meeker and Eels, 1949) to Gilbert (2003) in the U.S. and accounts such as Reid (1989) and Argyle (1994) in Britain, no clear method of identifying social membership has emerged. As Gilbert observes "there is as much art as science in the study of social stratification" (Gilbert, 2003: 16). For sociolinguists there is the added problem that the categories identified by sociologists or political scientists may not be the most useful for investigating language variation, which seldom receives attention from scholars in these fields.

There are two basic questions that are crucial in employing social class as an extralinguistic variable: (1) How many divisions are there within the category of social class? (2) How is membership in any of these divisions to be identified? The answer to both these questions will be affected by the degree to which social class is a salient category in the community. Milroy (2004) has pointed out that social class is a much more salient notion in Britain than in the U.S. The kinds of issues that are discussed in Britain with reference to social class are more often considered in terms of racial differences in the U.S. The extent to which social class differences are a common feature of public discourse will affect the ways in which membership in a particular category can be identified. I will illustrate this with an example from my own work.

When I was planning my work in Glasgow (Macaulay and Trevelyan, 1973; Macaulay, 1977), I knew that social class would be an important factor to investigate. At that time the most recent work on Scottish society was Kellas (1968) in which it was suggested that there were three major social class divisions in Scotland, based on occupation. In category I, Kellas included employers, managers, professionals, and farmers. In category II, he placed intermediate nonmanual workers, junior nonmanual, foremen and supervisors (manual), and skilled manual workers. In category III, he had semi-skilled and unskilled manual workers (Kellas, 1968: 39). In adopting this classification, I modified it by splitting category II by separating manual workers from nonmanual, because I believed that the difference between manual and nonmanual workers might be important for speech. This gave four social class groups. The Registrar-General's (RG) list of occupations provided a guide to membership in each of these categories:

- Class I   Professional and managerial (RG: 1,2,3,4,13)
- Class IIa   White-collar, intermediate nonmanual (RG: 5,6)
- Class IIb   Skilled manual (RG: 8,9,12,14)
- Class III   Semi-skilled and unskilled manual (RG: 7,10,11,15)

I used these categories to identify a judgment sample of speakers, balanced for gender and age (10-year-olds, 15-year-olds, and adults) and the use of five linguistic variables was correlated with these categories.[1] On the basis of the results of the analysis, I came to the conclusion that the variation indicated only three distinct social class groups: I, IIa, and IIb + III (Macaulay, 1977,

---

[1] Milroy and Gordon (2003: 31), following an error by Romaine (1980: 170), observe that my sample was not based on "objectively specifiable criteria but on the subjective assessment of an Inspector of Education." However, the Inspector of Education did not choose the sample but merely suggested the range of schools from which the sample would be chosen. The sample was chosen randomly from the school lists of father's occupation. There was no subjective selection of

1976b). In other words, the difference between manual (IIb and III) and nonmanual (IIa) workers proved important, a difference that would have been obscured if I had adopted the tripartite division suggested by Kellas (1968). It is interesting that in the revised edition of his book, Kellas (1980) omits the classification into three broad categories and replaces them with a table that has seven categories, including a distinction between skilled nonmanual occupations and skilled manual occupations. I have no idea whether in 1980 Kellas was aware of the change I had made in his original categories, since there is no reference to Macaulay and Trevelyan (1973) or Macaulay (1977), but the coincidence is intriguing. In an article on social class (Macaulay, 1976b) I had suggested that the evidence of social class differences from sociolinguistic surveys might be useful to other social scientists. It would be pleasing if this were an example of such a case, but alas there is no evidence to support it.

As part of the interview I had included questions for the adult speakers about the number of social class categories in Glasgow and where they would place themselves. Their responses were consistent with the notion of a three-part division (Macaulay, 1976b). My present view, however, is that most of the responses indicated membership in either middle-class (Class I) or working-class (Classes IIb and III). The speakers in category IIa in effect identified themselves as "in-betweens" similar to those in Eckert's study who considered themselves to be neither Jocks or Burnouts (Eckert, 1989, 2000). As one woman put it:

> Well I wouldn't call myself middle-class but on the other hand I would call myself middling. In other words, I'm not up there and I'm not down there. I just reckon I'm pretty average.
>
> (Macaulay, 1977: 63)

This speaker sees the middle-class as being "up there" and the working-class as being "down there," but she does not have a simple label for people like herself who are "pretty average." This comment illustrates the danger of taking a label such as "middle-class" literally. The Class I speakers also resisted the suggestion that they were "upper class" although they admitted that they belonged to the upper stratum of Glasgow society.

Responses such as this one and others collected in the Glasgow survey (Macaulay, 1976b) show that even when social class divisions are salient in the society, there may not be an adequate public language in which to label

---

the children to be interviewed. In view of the fact that Milroy (1980) and Gordon (2001) both used totally subjective samples ("friends of friends") in their studies, it is curious that they suggest "Macaulay's sample is open to legitimate challenge by any individual who feels prepared and qualified to make a rival assessment" (Milroy and Gordon, 2003: 31). Several proverbs cry out to be cited.

the differences. Nevertheless, the kind of subjective opinions elicited in the Glasgow survey can be useful in identifying how the speakers themselves perceive the critical social class divisions in a society. Perhaps investigators carrying out large-scale sociolinguistic surveys could incorporate some of the methods of perceptual dialectology (Preston, 2002).

Labov (1966) was able to make use of an earlier survey that had been designed by the New York School of Social Work for the Mobilization for Youth survey, with a team of forty interviewers. Labov drew a subsample from the 988 individuals who had been interviewed as part of the Mobilization for Youth survey. Probably, no other sociolinguist has had such a large randomly chosen sample to work with.

Labov made use of a 10-point socioeconomic class index developed for the Mobilization for Youth survey by John Michael (Labov, 1966: 211–217). Michael's scale is based on measures of occupation, education, and income. Labov points out that Michael gave "considerable attention to the problem of dividing the continuum of social class" (Labov, 1966: 216) and this was a problem for Labov too. Labov did not only correlate use of the linguistic variables with speakers from each of the ten points on the scale. Instead, he usually grouped the speakers into three or four social class groups and illustrated the difference this can make (Labov, 1966: 220–248). The most interesting of these is the difference between Labov's Figure 1 for the class stratification of the variable (r) (Labov 1996: 222) and his Figure 11 for the same variable (Labov 1966: 240). In Figure 1, Labov has three social class groups: 0–2 (the lowest group), 3–5 (the middle group), and 6–9 (the highest group). The three groups show the same stylistic variation, with steadily increasing use of /r/ with greater formality (i.e., attention to speech). In Figure 11, which is the most frequently cited example of hypercorrection, there are six groups: 0, 1, 2–3, 4–5, 6–8, and 9. The graph shows that the second highest group (6-8) use more /r/ in reading aloud minimal pairs than the speakers in the highest group (9).

This difference was concealed by the grouping in Figure 1. The example illustrates one of the problems with "dividing the continuum of social class." There is clearly a linguistic justification for the grouping in Figure 11, but is there other evidence that the speakers in, for example, category 8 belong with those in categories 6 and 7 rather than with those in category 9?

For the (dh) variable (i.e., the use of a stop or an affricate instead of a fricative in words such as *this* and *then*), Labov divides the continuum into three groups: 0–4, 5–6, 7–9. This produces a regular stylistic pattern (figure 15, Labov, 1966: 246). However, from the list of speakers who used either stops or affricates (Table 5, Labov, 1966: 259), there is an argument for dividing the speakers into only two groups 0–4 and 5–9. In the first group,

14 of the 46 speakers (30 percent) use stops or affricates, in contrast to the second group, in which only 2 of the 35 speakers (6 percent) use any stops or affricates, a highly significant difference) The point at issue is not whether Labov's division is the appropriate one but rather that there are often choices of this kind to be made and that the choice should be well-motivated.

Later Labov (figure 2, 1966: 274) shows that educational level accounts for this dichotomy: speakers with less than a 10th grade education have a much higher frequency of stops and affricates. However, rather than employ the division into two social classes, Labov goes on to develop a four-point social class scale on the basis of education and employment (Labov ,1966: 278) that shows a more regular distribution of the speakers from the lowest social class to the highest in their use of (dh). In a re-analysis of Labov's data Horvath (1985: 64–65) showed that gender was also a powerful determinant of (dh) and better helped to explain the deviant case of Nathan B. (Labov, 1966: 249–253). Chambers (1995: 55–57) points out that the use of fewer nonstandard variants of (dh) is an important feature of upwardly mobile speakers, suggesting that this variable is salient for such speakers.

I was able to get some information from the speakers in Glasgow as to where they would put themselves in the class structure (Macaulay, 1976b, 1977) because social class, as Milroy (2004) points out, is a salient feature of identity in Britain. Labov's questionnaire does not include any question of this sort, either because he did not think it was appropriate or because he thought his respondents might have difficulty in answering it, but it would have been interesting to see what kind of answers they gave.

Labov (2004) followed a similar strategy in the Philadelphia Neighborhood Study. On the basis of education, occupation, and residence value he developed a 16-point scale which he then divided into six social classes: Lower working-class, Middle working-class, Upper working-class, Lower middle-class, Upper middle-class, and Upper class. Labov later uses regression analysis to tease out the different effects of occupation, education, and residence value on the use of the variables (2001a: 183–186). He concludes that

The predominance of occupation for the most recent changes suggests that the combined index [i.e. the six social classes] is preferable only for those changes that have become engaged in the processes of sociolinguistic differentiation which extend over large portions of the speaker's life span. For young people growing up, the occupation of the breadwinner(s) of the family is the strongest determinant of their linguistic behaviour ...

(Labov, 2001a: 185)

This is consistent with Labov's earlier comment that "It is generally agreed that among objective indicators, occupation is the most highly correlated with other conceptions of social class" (2001a: 60). The other factors are perhaps more relevant to notions of social prestige in general than to categories of social stratification. It is hard to be sure from Labov's charts but there would appear to be a major difference between his first three groups (the working-class groups) and the other three (the middle-class and upper-class groups). In terms of social class differences, a two-way division would probably have provided very clear evidence of the difference between the two. Would this have been a more accurate picture of social class differences in speech than the one that Labov presents? In the absence of any corroborating evidence it is impossible to tell, but the question would be worth exploring if Labov's primary concern were with linguistic indicators of social class identity rather than with the process of linguistic change.

Trudgill (1974) also selected a quasi-random sample from the local register of electors from four of Norwich's electoral wards. Trudgill then developed a social class index on the basis of six separate indicators: occupation, father's occupation, income, education, locality, and housing. Trudgill scored each of these indicators on a six-point scale and added them together giving a range from 0 to 30 (1974: 38–44). One problem with this approach is that each of the indicators is taken to have an equal effect on social class (Macaulay, 1976b: 185) and that assumption may not be justified. In Warner's Index of Status Characteristics (Warner *et al.*, 1949), occupation was weighted 4, income 3, housing 3, and dwelling area 2. These weightings were developed on the basis of local research, but the results have been criticized as not measuring class (Argyle, 1994: 5).

Like Labov, Trudgill then, on the basis of linguistic data, grouped the scores on the 30-point range into groups that he labeled Middle middle-class, Lower middle-class, Upper working-class, Middle working-class, and Lower working-class. Trudgill was able to show fine stratification in these five categories, but a sceptic might wonder whether the separation of the working-class speakers into three categories is justified. Like Labov, Trudgill did not ask his speakers about social class or where they would put themselves, but as a native of Norwich Trudgill may have felt confident that they would have identified themselves according to the categories he established, even though they might not have used the same labels.

Labov (1966) and Trudgill (1974) used the scores for particular variables in setting up the discrete classes. Fontanella de Weinberg (1974) in her study of word-final -s in Bahia Blanca developed two scales, one based on occupation alone and one in which levels of education were taken into consideration. These scales provided different results and it is not clear which method most accurately reflects the social stratification (Macaulay, 1976b). It is not enough to have results that show a correlation unless there is reason to believe that the divisions revealed correspond to some social reality.

Other social categories

Given the complexity of dealing with social class, some investigators have followed the example of the Milroys (Milroy and Milroy, 1977; Milroy, 1980) in using social networks as the basis for examining language variation. Social networks are "personal communities which provide a meaningful framework for solving the problems of daily life" (Milroy, 2002: 550). A network approach "provides a set of procedures for studying small groups where speakers are not discriminable in terms of any kind of social class index" (Milroy, 2002: 556). This approach has been employed in a number of communities: Belfast (Milroy, 1980), Brazil (Bortoni-Ricardo, 1985); Austria (Lippi-Green, 1989), Detroit (Edwards 1992). In Louisiana Dubois and Horvath (1998) combined survey methods with social networks in their investigation of Cajun English.

Social networks are particularly effective in uncovering the interaction of factors such as gender and social class (Eckert, 2000) or membership in gangs (Labov et al, 1968; Fought, 1997). It also helps to avoid the dangers of essentialism "the (Aristotelian) reductive tendency by analysts to designate a particular aspect of a person or group as explanations for their behavior" (Mendoza-Denton, 2002: 476). For example, Milroy (1980) avoided the obvious social categories of Catholic and Protestant in her investigation of Belfast English.

Labov (2006: 399) points out that in Shana Poplack's Ottawa study network contacts were explicitly banned:

> This is not the result of prejudice against social networks, but rather from the recognition that members of the same social network are likely to be more similar to each other than to non-members. In that sense, a study that interviewed three social networks is a study of three extended individuals, and is not as likely to represent the community as a study of 100 individuals.
>
> (Labov, 2006: 399)

A similar kind of approach is to examine a community of practice. "A community of practice is an aggregate of people who come together around mutual engagement in an endeavor" (Eckert and McConnell-Ginet, 1992). Eckert (2000) demonstrates the value of this approach in her study of high school students in Detroit. The difference between a social network and a community of practice is not simply one of size, though networks have the potentiality to be much larger than communities of practice. One important difference is that an individual "may belong to or participate in a number of different communities of practice" (Meyerhoff, 2001: 531), while individuals are less likely to belong to numerous social networks.

Social networks and communities of practice provide an alternative basis for approaching language variation, but they do not replace the larger notions of age, gender, ethnicity, and social class, since individuals will still have these characteristics. As Milroy observes:

> Since no one claims that personal network structure is independent of broader social, economic, or political frameworks constraining individual behavior, a social network analysis of language variation does not compete with an analysis in terms of a macro-level concept such as social class.
>
> (Milroy, 2002: 550)

This, however, leaves the problem of making sure that the macro-level concepts are clearly defined and the categories well-motivated.

Questions for discussion

Of the four major social categories examined in the chapter, which do you consider the most likely to explain variation in any community?

In your community, which of the social categories do you consider the most salient for the study of variation?

Which of the major social categories do you consider to be the most difficult to define in operational terms?

Based on your reading of sociolinguistic reports, which of the social categories do you consider the most problematic for an investigation into linguistic variation?

How would define ethnicity in your community?

2 The Nature of Data

Behavior does not yield data by parthenogenesis. The role of the scientist in the process is to choose the genus; the behavior then chooses the species. Behavior never acts or speaks for itself in creating data; it only speaks, when spoken to, when asked a question.

(Coombs, 1964: 29)

Coombs (1964) points out that there is an ambiguity in the use of the word *data*: "The term is commonly used to refer both to the recorded observations and to that which is analyzed" (1964: 4). Coombs (1964: 4) provides a diagram to illustrate the difference. From what Coombs calls "the universe of potential observations," the scientist chooses to record certain observations. These recorded observations do not at this stage constitute data in Coombs' theory. The scientist must first convert these observations into data by classifying them into categories from which inferences can be drawn. Only then will it be possible for the scientist to begin the analysis of the data.

It is important to note, in the context of a book about speech, that Coombs' expression "recorded observations" does not refer to tape recordings but to what the scientist pays attention to. On the contrary, a tape-recorded interview would constitute an example of what Coombs calls "a universe of potential observations." From this universe, the scientist will decide to pay attention to certain things and ignore others. Coombs' example is that a political pollster asking an individual who he will vote for will probably not record how long it took the individual to answer, whether there was a change in respiration, or what he did with his hands, though in other situations (e.g., police questioning) these might be significant factors. In other words, the pollster will pay attention to some aspects of the situation (the response to the question) and ignore others. Similarly, the sociolinguist in attending to the tape-recording of an interview will pay attention to some details and ignore others.

For some studies, the data will consist of a transcript of a tape-recording and this is where Coombs' distinction becomes very clear. It is not unusual for linguists to refer to the tape-recording as data but that is not the way that

Coombs wishes to use the term. The tape-recording only provides the basis for the data that the analyst can extract from it. This is very obvious in the case of transcripts produced by different investigators for different purposes, which show the features that are of interest. Although the first two examples below are not from sociolinguistic studies, they illustrate different examples of data that can be extracted from a tape-recording. The conversation analysts (Sacks, Schegloff and Jefferson, 1974), for example, believe that the transcript should include a great deal of information that most sociolinguists will ignore. They include such information as details of pausing, audible in-breaths and out-breaths, and laughter, as in Excerpt 2.1:

Excerpt 2.1

Ken:	She's gotta jacket thet's diarrhea brhhhohhhwhnh. (0.8)
Ken:	'hhhhihh!(h)N(h)o j(h)oke. 'u- 'hhhihhh! Ri(h)illy. 'hhh It's ho:rrible. 'hhh Jis tuh'think about it. It gits you si(h)ck. (1.0)
Louise:	Yihknow it's almos' twenny e-it's um.

(Jefferson, Sacks and Schegloff, 1987: 161)

In Excerpt 2.1 the numbers in parentheses represent intervals of 'no speech' in tenths of seconds. The *h* symbol represents "discernable aspiration." The spellings are to give some indication of the sound of the word. For most sociolinguists much of this information is irrelevant and the time involved in transcribing a whole series of interviews in this way would be enormous. The conversation analysts' extensive use of idiosyncratic *eye-dialect* to suggest a certain style of production has generally been criticized by linguists (Preston 1982, 1985; Macaulay, 1991b) on the grounds that if details of pronunciation are to be shown it is better to use some accepted form of phonetic transcription. However, a total transcript in phonetic transcription is also impractical as was shown by Pittinger, Hockett, and Dahey (1960) in their book-length account of the first five minutes of an interview.

Chafe (1994), on the other hand, divides the transcript into intonation units, as can be seen in Excerpt 2.2:

Excerpt 2.2

A:	...(0.4) Have the .. animals,
	...(0.1) ever attacked anyone in a car?
B:	...(1.2) Well I
	well I heard of an elephant,
	...that sat down on a VW one time.
	...(0.9) There's a gir
	...Did you ever hear that?

C: ... (0.1) No
B: ... (0.3) Some elephants and these
    ... (0.1) they
    ... (0.7) there
    these gals were in a Volkswagen,
                    (Chafe, 1994: 61–62, slightly modified)

In this transcription, punctuation marks are employed to signal intonation. The comma indicates "a terminal contour which is not sentence-final," the period "a sentence-final falling pitch," and the question mark "a yes-no question terminal contour." Two dots mark "a brief pause or break in timing," and three dots "a typical pause (up to one second)." The numbers in parentheses show "a measured pause" (Chafe, 1994: xiii). As Chafe admits, this kind of transcription is very time-consuming, and it would be problematic for the presentation of long texts.

In my own transcripts for the purposes of examining narratives (Macaulay, 2005b), I employed a representation that roughly (but not always) corresponded to clauses, as in Excerpt 2.3:

Excerpt 2.3
(Dundee working-class woman)
the day that I—I went down to the station to meet him
when he was coming back
I thought
I'll meet him on the station
because after all these years in front of your mother and that you know
you—you wanted to—
the station was your privacy
                    (Macaulay, 2005b: 39)

There are many other ways of representing connected speech (Labov and Waletzky, 1967; Labov, 1972b; Hymes 1981, 1996; Tedlock, 1978, 1983; Gee, 1990; Dubois, Schuetze-Coburn, Cumming, and Paolino, 1993; Bucholz, 2000; Dressler and Kreuz, 2000; Fabb, 2002), and I have addressed the question of transcription elsewhere (Macaulay, 1991b, 2005b), but the point here is simply to illustrate the point that a tape-recording of speech is not data in Coombs' sense. O'Connell and Kowal also emphasize the need to make specific choices for each kind of investigation: "Since transcripts are tools for analysis and intelligibility, not cosmetic devices, they should include only what is relevant for a given research project" (O'Connell and Kowal, 2008: 94).

For many projects, however, a complete transcript is not necessary but there are still many decisions to be made in extracting the data from the tape-recording. Suppose, for example, that like Labov (1963) the investigator is interested in the diphthongs /ay/ and /aw/. One approach is to go through the tape and extract all the tokens of these diphthongs by identifying words that contain these sounds but it may turn out that some tokens are more revealing than others. One reason is differential stress. For example, the pronoun *I* and the interrogative *how* will sometimes be weakly stressed. They may also be quite frequent in the recordings. If all the tokens of this kind are included, this may affect the results. There is also the possibility that some speakers will produce more tokens of words with these two diphthongs than other speakers. Should the investigator ignore these differences and count all tokens? Or is it better to decide on a number that you can be fairly confident all speakers will use? If so, how is one to decide which tokens to include and which to leave out?

The investigator may decide, as I did in the Glasgow study (Macaulay and Trevelyan, 1973), to follow the example of Wolfram (1969:58) and include only a limited number of examples of each variable. In my study, I extracted the first 40 tokens of the variable from the first part of each tape and forty tokens from the second part. For the vocalic variables only examples in fully-stressed symbols were extracted but I excluded all occurrences before /r/. I also decided to include no more than three examples of any lexical item in case that biased the result. Horvath (1985) and Gordon (2001) follow a similar procedure. There is a danger in choosing the first *x* number of examples, as the speaker may be more relaxed later in the interview and use somewhat different forms. In Ayr (Macaulay, 1991a), I found that the use of a monophthong /u/ for the diphthong /au/ in words such as *house* and *down* was also affected by genre. Two of the speakers used more /u/ forms in narratives than in the rest of the interview (Macaulay, 1999). There were also examples of lexical items in idiomatic use that affected the frequency of the /u/ variant (Macaulay, 1999). So deciding which tokens to count is not a simple matter.

Trudgill (1974) did not limit the number of tokens of individual items that he extracted as can be seen from his Table 7.11 (Trudgill, 1974: 114), which lists the number of occurrences of the variant (o)-4 that occurred in FS (Formal Speech) and CS (Casual Speech) styles. Four words, *don't, only, suppose,* and *home* account for 80 percent of the tokens in FS and 77 percent of the tokens in CS, and *don't* alone constitutes 47 percent of the tokens. It is impossible to say what difference limiting the number of tokens of *don't* would have made (probably very little, since there are so many other words in the list) but the example illustrates the way in which a frequent lexical item might in some studies bias the analysis. Whatever method is chosen, the selection must be made on principled grounds so that the decision is not based on anything that might bias the results in the direction of an anticipated outcome. There is also a risk of bias if all tokens are extracted and significantly more examples are recorded from some speakers. Trudgill (1974) does not list the number of tokens extracted for each speaker. Labov (1966) gives examples of the number of tokens for a small number of speakers, and he comments on a problem where very few tokens of the variable (eh) were provided by one speaker (Labov, 1966: 117).

With morphological features, the same strictures apply. Wolfram (1969) in his investigation of word-final consonant clusters, tabulated the first 20 instances of monomorphemic clusters from one part of the interview, and the first 15 instances of bimorphemic clusters from the same part of the interview. If the same word occurred more than three times, only the first three examples were included. The most important decision was to omit tokens which occurred in a certain context:

> Clusters which were immediately followed by a homorganic stop (e.g., *test day*) were excluded from the tabulation since it was impossible to perceive from the tape-recordings whether the final stop was absent or present because of the phonetic environment.
>
> (Wolfram, 1969: 58)

This reference to the phonetic context in which the variable occurs is obvious in the case of consonant cluster reduction, but it may be important for phonological variables as well.

Wolfram (1993) later admitted that there was no clear justification for the choice of three instances:

> To be honest, I have no idea if three tokens for each word is an appropriate number for sampling the data, and I have since revised type-token procedures to be more sensitive to structural categories (e.g., three tokens for one word followed by a vowel, three when followed by a consonant, etc.) vis-à-vis simple, lexically based type-token considerations.... *Attention to lexical exceptions and type-token ratios must be considered in the extraction of data in order to ensure the most representative picture of actual variation.*
>
> (Wolfram, 1993: 214, emphasis in original)

Labov (1966) did not indicate the phonetic context of his variables, with the exception of the (eh) variable which is restricted to voiced stops (e.g. *cab*), voiced fricatives (e.g. *half*), and the nasals [m] and [n] (e.g. *ham, dance*). In the case of the interdental fricatives (th) and (dh) Labov did not distinguish tokens according to initial, medial, or final position, nor did he separate function words from other lexical items. (In his later work (e.g. Labov, 1994) he, of course, takes environmental effects into consideration.) Labov, however, collected four different kinds of data in New York. The first was connected speech as part of the interview. The other three involved reading: a connected passage, a word list, and a set of minimal pairs. The significance of these different kinds of data will be examined in Chapter 4. With the exception the use of the (t) variable by a sub-sample of ten speakers, Trudgill (1974) did not investigate the phonetic context in which the variables occurred. Trudgill found that for this sub-sample of speakers glottalization of (t) was more frequent in word-final position than in word internal position (Trudgill, 1974: 96). Trudgill followed Labov (1966) in classifying his data according to pre-determined stylistic categories.

In the Glasgow study, I distinguished the occurrence of glottal stops before a pause, before a vowel, and before a consonant (Macaulay, 1977: 47–8). The social class differences were greater before a pause or a vowel. Following an observation by Romaine (1975), I also found that glottal stops were more likely to occur before a vowel in the following word than before a vowel in word medial position. This supported Romaine's suggestion that word medial position was the most highly stigmatized position for glottal stops in Glasgow at that time.

For one of the vowel variables (i), the BIT vowel, I examined the preceding and following phonetic context to find out in what ways voicing, place of articulation, or manner of articulation affected the quality of the vowel for each of the social categories. I found that higher values of (i) (i.e. lower and more centralized variants) were found in conjunction with alveopalatals and preceding /h/, followed by bilabials and labio-dentals, then alveolars and velars. The lowest values of (i), i.e. the highest most front variants, were found when /θ/ preceded. What was most interesting, however, was that the results were consistent across age, gender, and social class groups:

> This shows that the phonetic factors affecting the quality of (i) are common to all members of the speech community and that the differences among groups must be due to non-phonetic factors.
>
> (Macaulay, 1977: 37)

As far as I know, this example of examining the impact of articulatory categories in the phonetic context of variables has not been followed in later studies, based on perceptual identification of the variants. Given that it was a lot of work and provided only negative information about social variation, this is hardly surprising. It was also probably doomed to failure. Thomas (2002: 169) points out that "impressionistic transcriptions of vowels in different contexts do not reflect the actual production of the vowel by a speaker as much as they reflect the scribe's perception." Unfortunately, according to Thomas, even phonetic training does not enable scribes to overcome their habitual practice of adjusting to the different acoustic signals which speakers produce to represent the "same" sounds. Kerswill (p.c.) disagrees and argues that if I could consistently hear these effects they were probably reliable. In their careful study of the transcription of consonants, using electropalatography, Kerswill and Wright conclude: "Segmental transcription using the IPA...is still the most succinct way of summarizing the relationship between the auditory and articulatory dimensions" (1990: 273). Thomas's comments, moreover, do not undermine Wolfram's point about the importance of type-token ratios.

Habick (1980), in a study of language change in Farmer City, Illinois, using spectrographic evidence, was able to show that "vowels under the influence of the palatals and velars are fronted more than those under the influence of labials" (Habick, 1980: 247). He observed that in active sound change "the fronting consonants pull the targets of back vowels under their influence further to the front than they normally do" (Habick, 1980: 248). Habick found that "it was seen in nearly every case that fronting affects back vowels that follow fronting consonants" whereas "back vowels that followed the backing consonants were usually less fronted or not fronted at all" (Habick, 1980: 249). He points out that this is consistent with the exceptions to the Great Vowel Shift which did not affect words such as *wound* and *stoop*.

Habick's use of spectrographic evidence follows Labov's shift from a perceptual method to an instrumental one (Labov, Yaeger and Steiner, 1972). Labov reports that "the two-formant plots have correlated well with impressionistic phonetics and increased the coders' confidence in their phonetic transcription" Labov (1994: 55). The major problem with instrumental measurement of sounds is that speakers have different-sized vocal tracts and therefore the absolute values of acoustic measurements from male and female speakers, for example, cannot be directly compared. Consequently, it is necessary to apply a normalization operation to compensate for these differences.

There have been various proposals for normalization (Iri, 1959; Hindle, 1978; Nearey, 1978; Syrdal and Gopal, 1986), but as Thomas (2002) observes, there is no clear solution: "All normalization techniques have drawbacks; choosing one is a matter of deciding which drawbacks are tolerable for the study at hand" (Thomas, 2002: 174). Labov (2001: 158) agrees that "there is no consensus on what a good solution to the normalization process would be" and illustrates the impact of three different normalization methods (Labov, 2001: 159–162). He explains his selection of logmean normalization as "the logical choice" for the Philadelphia neighborhood study. Presumably other investigators also choose their method on logical grounds but it is important to remember when comparing the results from different instrumental studies that the normalization techniques applied may not be the same in each case.

The use of instrumental measurements involves other decisions, such as at what point in the syllable to measure the vowel. Published reports of studies do not always include such information and it is principally of interest to other scholars who are engaged in similar kinds of measurements. There is also the assumption that the information represented by the first two formants is adequate for comparative purposes, though there is some evidence that the third formant may be important in certain cases. Representing just the first two formants makes the graphic display much simpler, but is that a good enough reason? Raising the question does not imply that the present procedure is inappropriate but it is intended to reinforce the notion that many methodological decisions are taken for practical reasons.

There is an added distance from the raw data in the instrumental approach. Many people who have heard the tape that Labov distributed to illustrate his Martha's Vineyard study (Labov ,1963) will have judged that they could hear the different phonetic distinctions that he illustrated. In a similar fashion, we tend to assume that if we heard the tapes that Labov (1966) or Trudgill (1974) recorded, we would hear much the same differences as they record. There are obvious dangers in relying on the perceptual acuity of the investigator(s), but there may be corresponding dangers in attaching importance to distinctions that show up instrumentally but are not audible to listeners (Thomas, 2002: 169).

The extension of quantitative methods to syntactic and other higher level features was hindered by the way in which linguistic variables were identified. Labov's notion of the linguistic variable was first stated in his New York study:

> The most useful items are those that are high in *frequency*, have a certain *immunity from conscious suppression*, are integral *units of larger structures*, and may be easily quantified on a linear scale.
>
> (Labov, 1966: 49, emphasis in original)

It is obvious that syntactic features do not fit this description and Labov goes on to say : "By all these criteria, phonological variables appear to be the most useful" (Labov, 1966: 49). Attempts to move beyond phonological and morphological features were further hampered by Labov's statement:

> Social and stylistic variation presuppose the option of saying "the same thing" in several different ways: that is, the variants are identical in referential or truth value, but opposed in their social and/or stylistic significance.
>
> (Labov, 1972a: 271)

As Lavendera (1978) pointed out this works fine for phonological and some morphological features, but is problematic for syntactic differences such as active versus passive or the differences between *get* passives and *be* passives. Lavendera proposed "to relax the condition that referential meaning must be the same for all the alternants and substitute for it a condition of functional comparability" (1978:181). This is exactly what some investigators have done, e.g., in the analysis of quotatives. Tagliamonte and Hudson (1999) list seven different verb forms (plus one miscellaneous category) that were used to introduce dialogue in narratives. These items illustrate the notion of "functional comparability" without requiring any specification of their meaning. The class of alternants is easy enough to identify, provided a sequence in the narrative is identified as "dialogue."[1]

In other cases, the class of alternants may be less constrained as in Cheshire's (2007) category of 'extenders,' that is, expressions such as *and everything, and that*, and *and stuff*. Both these examples illustrate the choice of a complex category as the linguistic variable.

It is also possible to take a different approach to data extraction. It has been normal practice for sociolinguists to identify a small number of linguistic variables and search the tapes for instances. As a consequence, much of the recorded speech is ignored. There is no way to judge how much information about variation in language has been ignored because investigators have been narrowly focused on a few variables. The corpus of Recorded Observations (in Coombs' sense) that could be extracted from the tapes collected in sociolinguistic studies is considerable; the amount of data that has been extracted from these tapes is regrettably much smaller. The extreme example is the Detroit Dialect Survey (Shuy, Wolfram and Riley, 1968a) in which more than 700 interviews were recorded but the only cases analyzed were those of "48 Negro informants" (Wolfram, 1969: 14). This is, however, only an extreme example. Many sociolinguistic studies (e.g. Milroy, 1980) make it clear that good examples of spontaneous speech were recorded, but only a few phonological variables are examined and the other aspects of language are ignored. Romaine (1984: 95) pointed out that there is a risk in dealing only with those aspects of linguistic structure that are easily quantifiable and ignoring those that are more difficult to deal with. Much of the motivation for this narrow focus has come from the obsession with linguistic change. Since it is easier to document changes in pronunciation than in syntactic or discourse features, most sociolinguistic studies have focused on the problem of sound change. This work has tended to neglect the notion of linguistic stability (Macaulay, 1988b) which is an equally interesting phenomenon. It is also the case that changes in syntactic and discourse features are less salient and require a different approach.

---

[1]Even with prosodic clues it is not always clear whether a sequence is to be identified as dialogue, but most cases are not problematic.

In my own work on syntactic and discourse variation, I have preferred to start from a complete transcript in an electronic text that can be easily searched and also provide a concordance. (As pointed out above, the form of transcription will depend upon the aims of the investigation.) The use of such a computerized text, however, differs in important ways from what has come to be known as Corpus Linguistics (e.g. Aijmer and Altenberg, 1991; Svartvik, 1992; Hunston, 2002). Corpus Linguistics generally deals with large corpora that have been collected by methods that do not make them appropriate for sociolinguistic investigation and the aims are to uncover patterns of distribution in general use rather than differences in usage. It is unlikely that many sociolinguists would subscribe to the notion: "Analysis should be restricted to what the machine can do without human checking, or intervention" (Sinclair, 1991: 381) since this would seriously restrict the number of variables to be investigated. There are some items that *can* be investigated this way since they are unambiguous and invariant. I was able to show that the distribution of *very* in Scottish speech was related to social class (Macaulay, 1991a, 1995, 2002). This is an example of an invariant form that is consistent in function and meaning (Macaulay, 2005a: 17). However, invariance of form and function is not enough. The word *quite* is invariant and consistent in function but it can be used either as a maximizer or a minimizer (Quirk, Greenbaum, Leech, and Svartvik, 1985). Sinclair's machine will find it difficult to distinguish these two uses, and human analysts will also sometimes find themselves in doubt. More complex variables will require more decisions by the analyst. In other words, the electronic text provides only the basis for relatively easy searching; it does not do the analyst's work.

My first venture was the examination of social class differences in twelve interviews in the town of Ayr (Macaulay, 1991a). I transcribed the interviews in their entirety and assigned a syntactic category label to each clause (Macaulay, 1991a: 21–22). This enabled me to compare the two social class groups in terms of their use of syntactic structures, but it involved going through the transcript line by line and deciding into which category the clause or phrase should be classified. It was a lot of tedious work and the electronic text only aided me by making it easy to count the number of each construction for each speaker. (The results are shown in the appendix to Macaulay 1991a.)

The analysis did not show great social class differences in syntactic patterns, although there were some interesting differences. The demonstration of few social class differences in syntactic features, however, is important for refuting pejorative claims such as those made by Bernstein (1962). The concordances of the interviews of the two social class groups also revealed an interesting difference in the use of adverbs, including the use of *very* (Macaulay, 1991a, 1995). This was not something that I had set out to investigate but it turned out to be a significant discovery that was confirmed by later studies (Macaulay, 2002, 2005a). It is an example of a finding that was not the result of a deliberate investigation of the possibility. The use of an electronic transcript of speech makes possible such unexpected discoveries. As Cheshire (1999) observes:

> In variationist analyses we are limited in what we discover by what we set out to look for; so it is hardly surprising that despite the emphasis of twentieth century linguistics on the primacy of speech, the field of language study that has worked more than any on the analysis of spontaneous speech has, paradoxically, discovered rather little about the syntactic features that characterize it.
>
> (Cheshire, 1999: 65–6)

Investigating discourse features requires a different approach to data extraction because many lexical items have multiple uses. For example, the word *well* is a frequent discourse marker (Schiffrin, 1987; Svartvik, 1980), but it must be distinguished from the use of the same form as a noun or an adverb. Extraction of examples of *well* as a discourse marker requires attention to the context in the utterance.

A more complex example is the discourse marker *you know*. This sequence can be used as part of a construction in which *you* is the subject and *know* is a finite verb, as in *you know where he lives*. This is quite different from the use of *you know* as a discourse marker in examples such as *I could see you know the hunted look on his face* and *you didnae offer her money you know*. A failure to distinguish between these two uses of *know* will distort the results.

An even more complex example is the form *like*. D'Arcy (2007: 392) distinguishes nine different uses of *like*: verb, noun, adverb, conjunction, suffix, quotative complementizer, approximative adverb, discourse marker, and discourse particle. No computer program is going to sort these out (Leech, 1997: 2); the analyst must simply go through and extract the items or mark the text. In either case, the computer will make it easy to tabulate the results but that could also be done by hand.

Finally, the worst case scenario for a simple computerized transcript is the phenomenon of zero forms. It is relatively easy to identify that a certain form has occurred. It is much more difficult to notice that something is missing. The obvious examples in English are restrictive relative clauses with no relative pronoun. There is probably no way to avoid going through the text marking all relative clauses and noting the presence or absence of a relative pronoun. A similar situation exists with complementizer *that*. In these cases, the best solution may lie in marking the transcript in some way to signal the zero form. In that way the instances can be easily retrieved. Having a computerized transcript is only a tool, like slide rule or a calculator; it does not provide answers by itself.

Coombs' Universe of Potential Observations is vast in the case of speech since it is such a fundamental aspect of our existence. The development of simple, efficient methods of recording speech has made the extraction of Recorded Observations relatively easy. The task of converting these observations into data remains a challenge for sociolinguists. The key to progress in the field is that the methods of extracting the data and the criteria employed should be clearly stated so that other scholars will be able to evaluate the results and make use of the examples.

In the Glasgow study (Macaulay, 1977) I included in an appendix the scores for all the speakers for all the variables. This enabled two scholars, Berdan (1978) and Cichocki (1988) to reanalyze the results (see Chapter 4). In my subsequent studies in Ayr (Macaulay, 1991a) and Glasgow (2005a) I continued this practice. This seems to me a basic requirement for any empirical work that bases its findings on quantitative measures. It is not enough to provide averages and percentages or other forms of statistical analysis of the data. The empirical basis of the claims is the raw data as extracted from the recorded observations. Without access to these numbers, everything has to be taken on trust. If there is no space available in the print version, the raw figures should be posted on the internet for interested scholars. In this way we can hope that our efforts will provide basis for future investigations.

Questions for discussion

Do you agree with Coombs' view that any recording of data is the result of choices made by the investigator?

Which form of transcription of recorded speech do you find best suited for the investigation of language variation?

Should all the tokens of a variable be counted or only an equal number for each speaker? Should the number of tokens for each word be limited?

What are the advantages and disadvantages of instrumental versus perceptual methods for measuring language variation?

How important do you consider the need for normalization in instrumental studies?

What different kinds of problems arise in investigating syntactic and discourse variation?

3 Collecting Data

Since we are constantly surrounded by examples of language use, both spoken and written, the opportunities for collecting evidence are extensive. What investigators choose to sample and how depends upon the question they want to answer. For example, those who are interested in language change before the era of acoustic recording are dependent on written records (Schneider, 2002). For certain kinds of syntactic, semantic, or lexical change, printed materials may be adequate (e.g. Rissanen, Kytö, and Heikkonen, 1997a,b) but changes in pronunciation are more difficult to chart and may involve the study of spelling variants in personal letters and journals, and comments made by the writers of guides to pronunciation at a particular time in the past. Similarly, changes in the present-day written language can be studied through the use of a wide variety of materials in both archival and electronic form (Biber and Finegan, 1988, 1989). As always, the questions that can be investigated will depend upon the availability of evidence. For example, it may be difficult to explore gender differences for some period in the past because of the paucity of examples from females (Kytö, 1997).

Most sociolinguistic investigations, however, concentrate on the spoken language at the present day, and most use some form of electronic recording. This is not essential, however. It is possible to collect observations by making notes of what you have heard. The best-known example of this is Labov's department store survey (Labov, 1966: 63–89). As part of his investigation of the use of post-vocalic /r/ in New York, Labov chose three department stores, Saks, Macy's, and Klein's, on the hypothesis that the use of post-vocalic /r/ by the sales staff in each of the stores would reflect that of their clientele, which he was able to demonstrate quite convincingly.

Labov chose an item which was sold on the fourth floor of the store, e.g., women's shoes, and asked a range of sales assistants the same question: "Excuse me, where are the women's shoes?" The usual answer would be "Fourth floor." Labov then leaned forward and said "Excuse me?" obtaining another, more emphatic repetition of the same information. He then moved away and made a note of the pronunciation of /r/ in the two tokens of *fourth* and *floor*. In this way, Labov obtained information on a key item from 264 individuals who had no idea that they had just been interviewed as part of a sociolinguistic investigation of New York speech.

Labov used this method to elicit specific forms but it is also possible to make notes on forms that occur naturally in unsolicited language interactions (Dubois and Crouch, 1975). This, in fact, may be the only way in which to collect evidence on such forms as greetings, apologies (Holmes, 1990), compliments and insults (Manes and Wolfson, 1981; Holmes, 1988), or service encounters (Coupland, 2000). One disadvantage of this approach is that the range of examples will be constrained by the extent of the investigator's social contacts, though that need not invalidate the evidence recorded. Another problem in observing strangers is that there may be inadequate information on the background of the speakers. Some characteristics, such as age and gender, may be relatively easy to deduce, but others, such as ethnicity, social class, and geographical origin, will be more difficult. Finally, in most cases of informal observations it will not be possible to make audio recordings, so the results will not be verifiable by others. There is also the risk that the recorded observations may be influenced by the investigator's expectations. Nevertheless, this method of collecting information can be valuable, as Labov and others have shown.

Most sociolinguistic studies, however, depend upon audio recording of speakers so that samples of their speech can be analyzed in depth and some features perhaps measured instrumentally. Some investigators (e.g. Goodwin, 1984; Ochs, Smith and Taylor, 1989; Vuchinich, 1990) have used videotaping but that involves complex and expensive arrangements and would be difficult to employ with a large sample. The major problems for sociolinguistic methodology are: (1) obtaining adequate samples of speech from a range of speakers in circumstances that are sufficiently similar to allow for meaningful comparison; and (2) deciding what to count. Both are common to all approaches to studies of language variation but when sociolinguistic investigation is extended beyond phonology and morphology they become even more critical. The question of comparability of samples is seldom discussed openly (Macaulay, 1978), provided that an adequate number of tokens of each variable can be tabulated, because the analysis usually deals with tokens extracted from their linguistic context. Recently some investigators have begun to look more closely at the context in which the tokens occurred (e.g. Rickford and McNair-Knox, 1994; Schilling-Estes, 1998, 2004) but so far they have dealt with individual interviews rather than any studies of a cross-section of the community.

The major challenge for sociolinguistic investigation, however, remains how to collect comparable samples of speech that can be used to chart the variation in a community. The principal method used so far has been the sociolinguistic interview (Labov, 1981). Despite adverse criticism (Wolfson, 1976; Milroy and Milroy, 1977), this method can provide valuable evidence not only of phonetic or phonological features but also syntactic and discourse features (Macaulay, 1984, 1991a; Schiffrin, 1987; Gregersen and Pedersen, 1991), particularly where the same interviewer conducts all the interviews so that there is some consistency in the approach to the interviewee. The role of the interviewer, however, is heavily biased in favor of being a receptive listener rather than an equal partner in the conversation between 'intimate strangers' (Gregersen and Pedersen, 1991:54). In an ideal sociolinguistic interview the interviewee is often a monologuist, telling stories, reminiscing, offering opinions, and so on. Clearly, individuals differ in the ways in which they take advantage of this opportunity (Macaulay, 1984, 1991a, 1999) and one of the important factors will be how the interviewee perceives and reacts to the interviewer (Macaulay, 1991; Schilling-Estes, 1998, 2004; Bailey and Tillery, 2004). This is not simply a matter of 'audience design' (Bell, 1984) since the contribution of both participants is critical and the interviewer's interest in and rapport with the interviewee can have an important effect on the quality of speech recorded (Macaulay, 1984, 1991a).

Interviews, however, do not give evidence of how speakers interact with their peers and limit the kind of genres and styles that can be recorded. For example, it is highly unlikely that joking and teasing will occur in an interview situation unless the two individuals know each other quite well, though occasionally interviewees will tell a joke, but that is a very different kind of speech act. Similarly, it is probable that many speakers will be using a form of speech appropriate in speaking to someone who is not a friend or an intimate. This can, though it need not, lead to rather formal or even unnatural speech (Wolfson, 1976; Milroy and Milroy, 1977). One way to counter this is to set up interviews with a group of speakers who know each other. Labov used this technique to record adolescents in Harlem (Labov, 1972b). The speakers were recorded through individual microphones on separate tracks, with the group as a whole recorded on a central microphone. The results were very impressive:

> The setting was essentially that of a party rather than that of an interview, with card games, eating and drinking, singing and sounding. The effect of observation and recording was of course present, but the natural interaction of the group overrode all other effects.
>
> (Labov, 1972b: xviii–xix)

This was an outstanding example of sociolinguistic research but it took considerable investment of time, energy, imagination, and resources to bring it to a successful conclusion. When a group in Copenhagen attempted to record adults in group sessions to contrast with individual interviews, they found that the adults were relatively ill at ease in the groups and their speaking style was generally more constrained than it had been in the individual interviews (Gregersen and Pedersen, 1991: 56). This is a good cautionary example of how a technique that works in one situation may be less effective in another. Macafee (1994) also reports on some problems that can arise in group situations.

One important advantage of the sociolinguistic interview is that speech can be recorded in relatively quiet surroundings and there is never any doubt whose voice is being recorded. In group sessions there is a much greater chance of extraneous noise and unless each speaker is recorded on a separate track from an individual microphone there is always a risk that it may be difficult to separate out the contribution of each speaker if their voices are not clearly distinct. It is also difficult to arrange a systematic set of group interviews by a stratified sample and the results, as in the Copenhagen study, may be disappointing because of the unnaturalness of the speech event for the participants. This makes it difficult to obtain comparable samples of speech, since if the speakers in one group feel more at ease than the speakers in another the resultant speech events may be very different.

Stenström, Andersen, and Hasund (2002) used a very different method in collecting data for the Bergen Corpus of London Teenage Language (COLT). Their aim was to investigate "the London teenage vernacular" (p. 3). They recruited 32 teenagers, aged 13–17, provided them with a Sony Walkman Professional tape recorder and instructed them "to carry this equipment for three to five days and record all the conversations they were engaged in, in as many different situations as possible, preferably with friends of their own age and, if possible, without any of the co-speakers noticing that they were being recorded" (p. 3). The intent of this method was clearly to collect as natural a sample of teenage speech as possible, but as Wolfson (1976) observed 'natural' is a complex notion in language. Stenström et al. point out many of the problems they encountered. Some of the teenagers recorded very little speech and often the quality of the recording was poor. The amount of speech recorded by each participant varied greatly. The situations in which the recordings were made also differed greatly.

There is perhaps a more fundamental problem with the methodology. Given the instructions the recruits received, there is no control over the kinds of speech events recorded. Since the nature of the speech event will affect the kind of speech recorded (Hymes, 1974), there is no guarantee that the samples of speech can be compared in a systematic way unless they consist of similar speech events (Macaulay, 2001b). The problem is clearly illustrated by those teenagers who chose to record classroom interactions where the principal speaker was the teacher and where the speech of the teenagers would be constrained by the situation. Similarly, some chose to record interactions with their parents and these samples would probably differ from the ways in which they spoke with their peers.

Equally important is the way in which the recruits approached the problem of recording their peers. Fortunately, from an ethical perspective, the recruits apparently did not indulge in much surreptitious recording, despite the instruction from the investigators, but their efforts to get their peers to record interesting speech may sometimes have distorted the situation. For example, there are indications that some of the recruits actively encouraged their interlocutors to swear on tape (Stenström, Andersen, and Hasund, 2002: 77–86). This raises doubts about the value of differences in the number of swear words recorded by different groups. Another example comes from a West Indian girl who provided a tenth of the corpus, thus biasing the sample of speech recorded. She is quoted as trying to get her friends to get into an argument on tape ("I want a fight on tape" p. 202). There is no great harm in provoking such speech events but it goes contrary to the notion of recording the conversations the teenagers were 'engaged in' (p. 3) in everyday situations. The COLT corpus clearly contains a great deal of valuable information on adolescent speech but there are problems with its usefulness for comparative purposes (see Chapter 6).

However, there is a form of recording that lies between the monologues of individual interviews and the polyphony of group sessions but is constrained to a single type of speech event. This is to set up a situation in which two speakers, who know each other and who are from the same kind of background, talk to each other in unstructured conversations in optimal recording conditions (Docherty, Foulkes, Milroy, Milroy, and Walshaw, 1997; Stuart-Smith, 1999). This avoids the danger of accommodation (Giles and Powesland, 1975) to the speech of an interviewer, perhaps from outside of the community (Douglas-Cowie ,1978) or from a different sector of the community (Rickford and McNair-Knox, 1994). Naturally, speakers may react differently to the artificiality of the situation but the method permits the systematic collection of extended samples of speech from a selected sample of the population, without the investigator's contribution affecting the interaction. This method comes close to overcoming the 'Observer's paradox' (Labov, 1972a). See Chapter 7 for an example of adolescent speech collected by this method.

Whatever form of recording is used, the aim is to obtain a data set that will provide materials for comparison between categories of speakers recorded under similar conditions and therefore appropriate for an analysis of any differences that may emerge. By examining a wide range of features it is then possible not only to plot differences in the use of such features that correlate with membership in extralinguistic categories such as social class, gender, and age, but also provide a baseline for comparison with studies of language variation in other communities. One of the goals of sociolinguistics should be to build a cumulative record of language variation in different communities to establish which kinds of variation are widely current and which restricted to particular types of community (Macaulay, 2003). Such a record might also help to identify the possibility that some interesting results are an artifact of the methodology employed.

Once the form of recording has been chosen, there are still decisions to be made. One is the location for the recording. Since extraneous noise can be a problem, a quiet location is obviously preferable but not always easy. Recording in the speaker's home has the advantage that the speaker may feel more at ease there than at another location but it is difficult for the interviewer to have control over noise from other family members (and the often intrusive television set). Young children may be a problem but, on the other hand, they may allow the interviewer to obtain samples of speech addressed to family members outside of the framework of the interview. For schoolchildren the school is the obvious location but this may constrain the type of language used to that considered appropriate for the classroom. That it need not do so is shown by the apparently uninhibited adolescent conversations recorded by Stuart-Smith (1999). (Some illustrations can be found in Macaulay, 2005a and in the appendix to the present volume.)

It is hardly surprising that two of the most successful investigations of adolescent speech (Cheshire, 1982; Eckert, 1989, 2000) were carried out by young women who were able to present themselves as close in age to the adolescents they were studying. (Cheshire also gained points with the adolescents by arriving on a motorbike.) Both projects, however, involved a commitment of time in participant observation much beyond the time spent in actual recording. As with Labov's study of Harlem adolescents, it was necessary to build up a comfortable relationship with the speakers to obtain a suitable speech sample. This kind of approach has not been generally employed in studies of adult speech though Lesley Milroy used network contacts in Belfast (Milroy, 1980) to gain access to working- class speakers in three communities and became involved in various activities with members of the families she met. Feagin (1979) used family connections to build up a network from which she selected the interviewees for her investigation of Anniston, Alabama. Sociolinguistic studies that involve ethnographic work of this kind require an extensive commitment of time that may not be feasible for many investigators but the benefits are considerable.

The most common form of sociolinguistic investigation has been to record interviews with a cross-section of the population, either mainly by a single interviewer (e.g. Labov, 1966; Trudgill, 1974; Macaulay, 1977), or by a team of interviewers (e.g. Shuy, Wolfram, and Riley 1968a; Gregersen and Pedersen 1991). To achieve comparability it has been common to employ a questionnaire in which the same questions are asked of all speakers, though different questionnaires are needed for children and adolescents, if they are part of the sample. The questionnaire can be used to elicit important information on the speaker's background and attitudes, but there is a trade-off. The more specific and detailed the questions are the greater the probability that they will be answered economically giving just the information requested. This can lead to what the Milroys have labeled 'interview style' in which:

> ... the two-part structure of the discourse is particularly evident, with the fieldworker eliciting and the informant replying ...
> ... interview style is characterized by slow pace with pauses between turns, no interruptions, and little fluctuation in tessitura and loudness.
>
> (Milroy, 1980: 66)

Labov (1966: 92) labeled this style 'careful speech' which

> ... is the type of speech which normally occurs when the subject is answering questions which are formally recognized as 'part of the interview.'
> Generally speaking, an interview which has as its professed object the language of the speaker, will rate higher on the scale of formality than most conversation.
>
> (Labov, 1966: 92)

Labov contrasted 'careful speech' with what he called 'casual speech' and he gave five contextual situations in which casual speech might occur (see Chapter 4).

Labov also used paralinguistic cues to identify casual speech in the five contexts listed above. Wolfram (1969) and Macaulay (1977) found it difficult to use these cues in any objective and reliable way, so that they did not employ the distinction between casual and careful speech in their analysis. More importantly, Labov used a reading passage and two word lists to focus more attention on the speech form. One of the theoretical problems with the 'attention to speech' approach concerns the use of materials to be read out loud as representing increasing attention to speech. As several investigators (e.g. Milroy, 1980; Romaine, 1980; Macaulay, 1999) have pointed out, there are problems in treating speech and reading aloud as a continuum (see Chapter 4).

Labov developed the notion of isolating different speech styles to provide a range of information within a single interview. It should be remembered that Labov had told his speakers that the purpose of the interview was to find out about language "and that the only object of the questions was to find out how the informant talked in every-day life" (Labov, 1966: 141). To minimize the inhibiting effect of the recording situation, Labov employs a number of strategies designed to put the interviewee at ease, including the interviewer trying to appear in a subordinate role as a learner (Labov, 1981). There is an ethical question about the extent to which the investigator should reveal the purpose of the study. Obviously, one cannot record people without their cooperation and all scholars reject the notion of surreptitious recording, but there may be a cost to complete disclosure in that it may lead to more refusals. Some investigators have resorted to mild deceptions by not emphasizing the linguistic nature of their interest. For example, Cheshire believed that in her approach to adolescent boys at an adventure playground she had to conceal her true purpose:

> It was essential, however, if natural spontaneous speech was to be obtained, for the boys not to know that their language was the object of study. I told them, therefore, that I was a university student and that I had a vacation job helping in research to find out what people in Reading thought of the town.
>
> (Cheshire, 1982: 14)

It turned out that she need not have worried and at the next playground she did not bother to fabricate a story.

In my own study in Glasgow (Macaulay and Trevelyan, 1973), I presented my interest as in social change, though it must have been clear to most people from many of the questions asked that I was very interested in language. Since the purpose of the project was not simply to collect samples of people's speech but also to investigate the importance of language differences in education and employment, I did not feel that I had deceived them greatly, but in retrospect I feel that I should have been more open with the speakers, at least when I had finished the interview. As Rampton (1992) points out, there can be benefits in telling people exactly what you are interested in and getting their cooperation in discussing the issues.

One of the difficulties involved in full disclosure is that most people will not be familiar with the aims of sociolinguistic investigation and it may be hard, particularly with middle and upper class speakers, to convince them that their form of speech is appropriate for intensive study. Whatever approach is adopted will affect the kind of questions asked and the attitude adopted by the interviewer. The researcher has to weigh the costs and benefits of the choice as well as the ethical issues.

In some situations it may be possible to record people surreptitiously, informing them afterwards and offering to erase the tape if they have any objections. Coupland (1988) enlisted the cooperation of an assistant in a travel agency and arranged to record her talking with clients. The assistant knew that she was being recorded but the clients did not. Before they left, Coupland approached the clients and told them about the recording, offering to erase the tape if they wished. Only four did or had any complaint about the situation. However, the clients had been recorded in a very public trans- action which anyone could have heard and presumably there was nothing embarrassing or confidential on the tape. In other situations the revelation of surreptitious recording may come as more of a shock. When Coates (1996) told her friends that she had secretly been recording their conversations, they were at first upset but later forgave her.

The extent to which the investigator can be open about the aims of the research may also depend upon the variety being studied. McCafferty (2001: 14–15) believed that it would have disrupted his interviewing in (London) Derry if he had been more open with people about his interest in ethnic differences. Rather than asking direct questions about sectarian differences, he restricted himself to mundane topics, knowing that references to more controversial matters would inevitably crop up.

People who are aware of speaking a dialect (or language) that is different from that of mainstream society will be very conscious of linguistic differ- ences and be able to comment on them. Such speakers are unlikely to be surprised that the investigator is interested in their speech. The method of traditional dialectology (Wilson, 1923; Orton, 1962) was to seek out older, rural speakers (usually males) who were recognized as genuine dialect speak- ers and who were willing to act as informants. It may be more difficult to get those who live in complex urban communities to talk about linguistic differ- ences, though it is possible to investigate attitudes towards different varieties by direct questioning (Preston, 2002).

Audio recording takes time to collect and much more time to analyze, so that the number of respondents is limited by the resources available. It is also dangerous to be too ambitious. There are cautionary examples in the literature of projects that collected more material than could be adequately analyzed at the time (Shuy, Wolfram, and Riley, 1968a; Pellowe et al. 1972; Jones-Sargent 1983). The Newcastle materials have now been transcribed and digitized by the NECTE project and are available online for future research. There is another method of obtaining data without the commitment of time that recording involves: postal questionnaires. Although postal surveys are most effective for collecting lexical information (Mather and Speitel, 1975–1986), postal questionnaires can also be used to collect some kinds of information on syntactic, morphological, and phonological variation, but not on fine-grained phonetic information (Nylvek, 1992; Chambers, 1994). Information on pronunciation, for example, can be gained by asking respondents whether they pronounce *route* to rhyme with *doubt* or *loot*.

Another source of information on language use is to be found in the mass media. Call-in talk shows and other forms of audience participation can provide examples of unscripted language but demographic information on the speakers may be unreliable. For example, there is no guarantee that a speaker from a given area grew up there and thus represents the speech of that area. However, it would be possible to explore some questions, such as age or gender differences, in this way. Archival recordings can also provide information on language change (Sankoff, 2004; Elliott, 2000).

Finally, the improvement in the quality of telephone communication has made it possible to obtain good recording in this way. The telephone survey of the Phonological Atlas of North America (Labov, Ash, and Boberg, 2006) has interviewed 762 speakers by telephone across the United States. This is a massive project that provides a comprehensive picture of pronunciation in North American urban areas. It would, however, be possible to conduct much smaller scale projects in this way. Labov's Philadephia study, for example, interviewed 60 speakers by telephone to supplement the face-to-face interviews (Labov, 2001).

It would be difficult to cover in one short chapter all the methods of data collecting that have been used in sociolinguistic projects but the examples will give some idea of the range of approaches. The opportunities for collecting data are manifold but the choice of methods will depend upon a number of factors affecting the design of the project as a whole. As Sankoff has pointed out:

> As we move into syntactic, lexical, and especially discourse-level variation, however, it becomes increasingly important to allow for idiosyncratic and situation-specific behaviour.
>
> (Sankoff, 1988: 903)

The development of new techniques for collecting samples of speech from a stratified sample of speakers is an important task for sociolinguists.

Questions for discussion

What are the advantages and disadvantages of different methods of data collection?

Which method would you employ in a survey of your community?

How would you address the problem of recording comparable samples of speech from a group of speakers?

How important do you consider the notion of 'full disclosure' to those whose speech you want to record? Are there any situations in which you would consider recording speakers surreptitiously?

What kinds of information on linguistic variety can effectively be collected through the use of written questionnaires?

4 Tabulating the Results

Labov (1963) set the model for many future studies by assigning a numerical value to each occurrence of the diphthongs (ay) and (aw) on a four-point arithmetical scale 0–3. For each speaker, he calculated an index of centralization by taking the mean of the numerical values for each diphthong and multiplied the result by 100. He then averaged the values of the indexes for members of social groups. This provides an unweighted mean in which "each individual contributes equally to the group mean, regardless of the amount of data collected from him" (Berdan, 1975: 83). This contrasts with a weighted mean in which "each observation or utterance contributes equally to the group mean" so that "an individual's contribution to the mean is weighted proportional to the amount of data available for him" (Berdan, 1975: 85). If the same number of tokens is extracted for each speaker, there will be no difference between a weighted and an unweighted mean, but if more tokens are extracted for some speakers than for others, the weighted mean will reflect the influence of those with more tokens. Most studies report unweighted means though in some cases it is not clear that this is so. In situations where some speakers produce very few tokens of a variable, the unweighted mean may be distorted by their contribution. For this reason (and others) it is helpful when the number of tokens extracted is given.

In the New York study, Labov (1966) used a six-point scale for each of the two vowel variables. In Norwich, Trudgill (1974) employed scales from two to five values for the vowel variables. In the Glasgow study, (Macaulay, 1977), I used scales of three to five values. In each of these studies the assumption was that since vowel variation is on a continuum, it is necessary to divide that continuum at arbitrary points in order to provide a basis for quantitative analysis. The resulting analysis in each study provided figures that could be correlated with social factors, but would the results have been different if the scales had been different? Speaking only for myself, I believed at the time that if the analysis showed interesting correlations, then *post hoc* it was validated. In retrospect I am not so sure. Romaine (1975) criticized my decision to treat the (au) variable (i.e. the vowel in words such as *down* and *house*) as a continuous variable rather than as a dichotomized one between a monophthong and a diphthong. I did so in the belief that some middle-class

41

speakers who would not typically be expected to use a monophthong might have centralized variants, and this turned out to be the case. However, the pattern of social stratification would probably have been much the same if I had included all the diphthongs in one category. In my later study of Ayr, (Macaulay, 1991a), I treated the variable as a simple dichotomy between a diphthong and a monophthong, and that provided enough information for both social and stylistic variation (Macaulay, 1999).

Milroy (1980) used a five-point index scale for one vocalic variable and three-point scales for two others. (The other variables were calculated as percentages.) Gordon (2001) in his study of the Northern Cities Shift created indices based on the degree of shifting (backing and/or lowering) but also carried out separate analyses of backing and lowering. Eckert (2000) identified from four to seven variants for the vocalic variables.

All these studies used the listing of the variants on an arithmetical scale to produce unweighted indices for categories of speakers. As far as I can tell, most investigators, with the exception of Labov, made no attempt to ascertain the extent to which the variants on the scale were perceptible to members of the community. Labov's Self Evaluation Test (Labov, 1966: 455–74) comes close to the kind of commutation test that shows whether two variants were perceived as the same or different. Labov was interested in the difference between the speakers' self-reported use of a variant and their actual use in the interview, but the results suggest that in many cases the speakers had difficulty in recognizing the differences.

In contrast to earlier studies, Horvath (1985) analyzed the variables in terms of discrete categories (e.g. Broad, General, and Cultivated) and through a Principal Components analysis (see Chapter 6) assigned speakers to sociolects which were then correlated with social categories. This method avoids the calculation of mean values for social groups but also obscures the differences between them, since the division into sociolects is made by dividing the continuum at arbitrary points.

Labov, Yaeger, and Steiner (1972) introduced a new approach. Instead of creating group indices, they illustrated the variation by presenting examples of individuals, showing diagrams of instrumentally measured vowels. Labov (2001) was able to apply this method to a diverse sample of Philadelphia speakers, showing age, gender, and social class differences in the use of six vocalic variables. As pointed out in Chapter 2, this process requires a normalization method to compensate for differences in vocal tract size and shape. Some investigators have also questioned the dependence on Formant 1/Formant 2 displays, since the third formant may also contribute importantly to some vowels, and duration may be important in other cases (Foulkes and Docherty, 1999; Thomas 2002). The effect of lip-rounding is also difficult to represent. Most instrumental studies have dealt only with vowels but increasingly investigators have been examining consonants (Foulkes and Docherty, 1999; Stuart-Smith, 1999). An example of a recent variationist study which relies entirely on spectrographic analyses to produce group indices is (Kerswill, Torgersen and Fox, 2008).

Spectrographic analysis has added greatly to our knowledge of linguistic variation, but it is unlikely to replace auditory analysis completely. Although the reliability of auditory judgments may be challenged, there are some advantages in that they have been made by a researcher familiar with the range of speech used within the community. Instrumental analysis sometimes reveals differences that are not apparent auditorily (Foulkes and Docherty, 1999). It is not obvious how important this is for understanding variation in the community. As Milroy and Gordon (2003: 151) point out in their discussion of auditory versus instrumental analysis: "The challenge for all researchers lies in establishing that the differences identified by the analysis are in fact the same ones that are relied upon by members of the speech community."

The emphasis in much sociolinguistic investigation has been on linguistic change and this has influenced the kind of features that have been examined. It has also affected the way in which variables have been extracted and analyzed. One of Labov's major achievements in his New York study (Labov, 1966) was a method of investigating stylistic change within the context of a single interview. Labov established a framework in which he distinguished between 'casual speech' and 'careful speech.' He started from the assumption that for most of the interview the speaker would use what he called 'careful speech' but that there were situations in which the speaker might relax into a more informal style. Labov identified five contextual situations for casual speech: (1) Speech outside the formal interview; (2) Speech with a third person; (3) Speech not in direct response to a question; (4) Childhood rhymes and customs; and (5) 'Danger of Death' narratives. These five criteria combine the effect of addressee and of topic. Labov used paralinguistic cues to identify casual speech in these contexts. According to the figures given for five speakers (Labov, 1966: 113–22), Labov identified from 16 percent to 37 percent of interviews as representing 'casual speech.' This is an impressive achievement and probably reflects Labov's skill as an interviewer in setting the speaker at ease. Trudgill (1974) also made a distinction between 'casual speech' and 'formal speech' but does not give any indication of the proportions in his interviews. Wolfram (1969) and Macaulay (1977) found it difficult to use these cues in any objective and reliable way, so that they did not employ the distinction between casual and careful speech in their analysis.

Labov also had three reading tasks: two connected texts, three word lists, and a minimal pairs test for the variable (r). Labov used the results from the two spoken styles and the various reading tests to treat them as a continuum reflecting increased attention to speech. Labov's focus on the attention paid to speech follows from his notion of the *vernacular*, which he defines as "that mode of speech that is acquired in pre-adolescent years," in which "the minimum attention is paid to speech," and which he claims "provides the most systematic data for linguistic analysis" (Labov, 1981: 3). There are problems with this definition of the vernacular (Reah 1982; Romaine 1984; Macaulay, 1988a).

One of the theoretical problems with the *attention to speech* approach concerns the use of materials to be read out loud as representing increasing attention to speech. As several investigators (e.g. Milroy, 1980; Romaine, 1980; Macaulay, 1999) have pointed out, there are problems in treating speech and reading aloud as a continuum. Milroy and Milroy (1977) showed that deletion of (th) was almost non-existent in word list style in Belfast even in those speakers who showed extremely high rates of deletion in spontaneous speech. They argued that the occurrence of (th) in the word list style was probably the result of the influence of the orthographic form. The evidence from reading in Labov's study would be much stronger if the written form contradicted the prestige pronunciation (e.g. *r*-lessness in RP). If the prestige form in New York had been *r*-lessness (as in London) and if the speakers had *increased* their deletion in the reading exercises, this would have been a more convincing demonstration that the results were not an artefact of the orthographic form. The fact that the results for the three consonantal variables (r), (th), and (dh) are all consistent with the written form makes the influence of orthography highly plausible.

The evidence from the vowel variables is less clear, but even there the influence of the written form cannot be ruled out. As Chambers observes in a study of the acquisition of British speech forms by six Canadian children: "In the early stage of dialect acquisition, features which are orthographically transparent progress faster than features which are orthographically opaque" (1988: 662). The influence of alphabetic literacy on phonological perception is still unclear but there is enough evidence to suggest that the relationship is problematic (see the discussion in Vihman, 1996: 174–82; Mann, 1986). Yet there has been little general recognition that, for example, the most frequently cited evidence for 'hypercorrection' in Labov's class stratification of (r) (1966: 240) comes largely from the assumption that reading aloud styles are part of a continuum with speech, and even thirty years later differences between speaking and reading aloud are still cited as evidence for different "speech styles" (e.g. Dailey-O'Cain, 1997).

Labov (2001) introduces a different approach to distinguishing between "casual speech" and "careful speech" within the interview by adopting what he calls a Decision Tree. This is based on the content of the speech produced by the speaker. Characterized as "casual" are narratives, speech addressed to someone other than the interviewer, talk about kids' games and experiences, and what Labov calls "tangents" when the speaker takes off on a topic not suggested by the interviewer. In contrast to "casual speech" the categories of "careful speech" consist of "response," which is the speaker's first sentence following something the interviewer has said, any remarks about language in the later section of the interview, and what Labov calls "'soapbox style", that is "an extended expression of generalized opinions, not spoken directly to the interviewer, but enunciated as if for a more general audience" (Labov 2001: 91). Any other speech not counted as casual is included in the category of careful speech. This is an interesting attempt to operationalize stylistic variation but it suffers from the basic problem with approaching style as a question of "attention to speech." There is no independent measure of attention. Nolan and Kerswill (1990) present an experimental design to isolate "style" and "attention to speech."

There are three major problems with this kind of approach to the study of stylistic variation:

1. Attempts to treat stylistic variation as unidimensional are unrealistic because any suggested explanation for the variation may be vitiated by factors that have deliberately been ignored.
2. It is essential to consider the significance of the written language in relation to the notions of prestige form and standard language.
3. Concentrating on what one interlocutor does without paying equal attention to what the other participant(s) may be doing cannot provide a coherent explanation of the speaker's behavior.

A different approach to the quantification of stylistic variation is the *audience design* theory of Bell (1984). Rickford and McNair-Knox (1994) list 23 studies that examined stylistic variation that seemed to depend on difference in the person addressed. Rickford and McNair illustrate the effect of change of addressee by contrasting the use of language by Foxy, an African-American teenager, in two very different interviews. In interview III Foxy was interviewed in her home by a forty-one-year-old African American woman (McNair-Knox) and her sixteen-year-old daughter, Roberta. In interview IV Foxy was interviewed by a twenty-five-year-old European American woman who was a graduate student. In a wide range of measures of African American Vernacular English, Foxy used significantly more of them in interview III than she did in interview IV. Rickford and McNair-Knox interpreted this stylistic shift as supporting Bell's notion of audience design. However, a major problem with Bell's model is that it minimizes the role of the addressee. This is not surprising since what Bell himself calls "the most striking case"

(1984: 171) is the stylistic shift he recorded for four newscasters on two New Zealand radio stations. In this case, it is quite reasonable to attribute the variation literally to audience design, since the broadcasters are presumably trying to reach out to their likely audience.[1] However, this audience is totally passive. There is no immediate feedback to the speakers and there can be no "accommodation" to changes that occur in the course of the speech event. In face-to-face encounters the course of the interaction is mutually negotiated by the participants. A failure to understand this fully underlies the views of those (e.g. Wolfson, 1976; Milroy and Milroy, 1977) who adversely criticized the quality of speech obtained through dyadic interviews. (For an argument in defence of interview data, see Macaulay, 1984, 1991a.)

When Rickford and McNair-Knox contrast Foxy's use of language in interview III and in interview IV, they seem to assume that the two speech events are equivalent. From an examination of the two situations this assumption is unjustified. In interview III Foxy participated in a three-way conversation with two people she knew, one of them her own age. In Interview IV Foxy participated in a dyadic exchange with a stranger, ten years older of very different background and education. It is clear from what Rickford and McNair-Knox say that the use of language by *all three participants* in Interview III was very different from that of both in Interview IV, and that Foxy was much more at her ease in Interview III. To call these equivalent speech events just because they come under the name 'interview' is misleading. To say that the only difference between these two speech events lies in the nature of the addressee is to ignore what Bakhtin (1981), Goffman (1981), Gumperz (1982), Hymes (1974), and others have said about speech events. There is, however, one section of Interview IV where Foxy apparently felt more at ease, that is the 12 percent of the transcript devoted to what Rickford and McNair-Knox call the topic "wives, slamming partners", a topic that also takes up 12 percent of Interview III. If we treat these two sections as equivalent (instead of treating the interviews as a whole as the basis for comparison), then there is no style-shifting and no addressee effect. Contrary to supporting Bell's thesis, it is a counter-example. Foxy uses the same kind of language (in terms of the features tabulated by Rickford and McNair-Knox) in speaking to a complete stranger of different race as she does in speaking to Faye and Roberta.

However, it would be unwise to attribute the stylistic change solely to topic shift. Bell (1984: 181) argues that that topic shifts can *cause* style shifts. This

---

[1]Paradoxically, the listening audience would seem to fit Bell's notion of referee (1984:186) better than audience, since referees are third persons not physically present at an interaction, but whose importance is so great that they influence speech at a distance.

is too mechanical an explanation. A topic shift may coincide with a change in the dynamics of the interaction and lead to style shifting, as it apparently did in the case of "wives, slamming partners" for Foxy, but change of topic may have little or no effect, as illustrated by several of the other eleven topics identified by Rickford and McNair-Knox (1994: 259–60).

The importance of topic (or genre) was recognized by Labov from the start. In addition to extending the stylistic dimension in the direction of greater formality through reading tasks, Labov (1966: 107) had sought to increase the amount of "casual speech" by encouraging the speaker to recall childhood rhymes and customs, and by the "Danger of death" question. Trudgill (1974), Macaulay (1977), and Milroy (1980), for very different reasons, found the latter to be a less successful question than Labov had experienced. In later interviews (Macaulay, 1991a), I found that while it sometimes provoked good narratives, these narratives were no different in style than those stimulated by, for example, questions about first job or meeting one's spouse. Gal (1979) points out that emotion-laden narratives (such as those elicited by the danger-of-death question) did not necessarily lead to the use of more dialect features in her interviews:

> We can hypothesize that from an Oberwarter's point of view, dialect features, when used to a standard speaker, primarily convey the speaker's peasant status and not his or her involvement in the narrative. It might even be supposed that, to impress a standard-speaking stranger with the importance of an emotion-laden incident, the Oberwarter would strain toward the standard to maximize intelligibility and convey seriousness in the listener's own terms; that is, in the linguistic variety most likely to be meaningful for the stranger.
>
> (Gal, 1979: 94)

What this comment underlines is that neither topic alone nor the status of the addressee determines stylistic choices but rather how the interlocutors perceive and categorize the situation and their awareness of the norms that apply to this situation. As Brown and Fraser point out

> ...a doctor consulting a lawyer on a legal question might well express deference in formulating his query, whereas the lawyer when consulting the doctor about his heart condition would be the one to express deference. ...So an understanding of the nature of the scene, *as viewed by the participants*, is essential in order to detect and interpret many of the markers that appear in their speech.
>
> (Brown and Fraser, 1979: 54, emphasis added)

Bell's theory of style as audience design is a more subtle form of "speech accommodation theory" (e.g. Giles and Powesland, 1975; Thakerar, Giles, and Cheshire, 1982). Accommodation theory describes the conditions under which the speaker's form of speech will "converge on" or "diverge from" the form of speech used by the addressee (or assumed to be used by the addressee). Bell takes this further by considering the effect not only of the addressee but also of auditors, overhearers, and eavesdroppers. Bell emphasizes that most speech is responsive to the audience (i.e. convergent) but may, under certain circumstances, initiate a different style (divergent). Bell supports his argument with examples taken from studies by Douglas-Cowie (1978) and Coupland (1980, 1988).

Douglas-Cowie tape-recorded ten inhabitants of a small village in Northern Ireland under two sets of conditions. The first was talking together in pairs (and with Douglas-Cowie herself); the second condition was talking one-to-one with an English outsider. Douglas-Cowie was able to show that the speakers tended to use more "standard" forms when speaking to the English outsider; however, this switch was less obvious in the second half of the sessions. Moreover, some speakers showed little or no change in certain variables, and a greater difference among the speakers was shown by their position on a Social Ambition scale. So, although Douglas-Cowie's results support Bell's position on audience design, they do so only weakly.

Jones-Sargent observes that Labov assumes "social ambitiousness to be the central cause of variation" (1983: 15) although there is no attempt to establish the validity of social ambition as the sole motivating force. All versions of the accommodation model, including Bell's, assume that questions of motivation are unproblematic. Bell also discusses what he calls "referee design":

> Referees are persons not physically present at an interaction, but possessing such salience for a speaker that they influence speech even in their absence.
>
> (Bell, 1984: 186)

Bell chooses to emphasize that referees are persons because he wishes to bring all stylistic variation under the general rubric of audience design but it is clear from his examples (e.g. RP as a model for prestige broadcasting in New Zealand) that he is actually talking about abstract norms. The problem with audience design as the sole explanation of stylistic variation can be seen in a query Bell himself raises:

> If the basis of style shift is addressee design, then the question of shift by upper-class speakers becomes an issue. Everyone else is shifting

towards them, but who can they be said to be shifting towards in formal speech?

(Bell, 1984: 199)

The answer seems obvious enough. The upper-class, like many other speakers (but not all), shift in the direction of the standard language, i.e. the written norm.[2] This is the probable explanation for the lack of low level phonetic processes in upper-class speech (Kroch, 1978), as much as for the difference between spoken styles and reading styles in Labov's New York study. Because consonant deletion and elision are seldom indicated in written language, it appears to many people as self-evident that the "correct" form of spoken language does not include such processes.

Sociolinguists seem to have been generally uninterested in the phenomenon of "allegro speech" (Zwicky, 1972), although this may be an important type of variation. Paul Kerswill is an exception, having examined allegro speech within a variationist analysis (Kerswill, 1987; Kerswill and Wright, 1990; Nolan and Kerswill, 1990).

Bell's notion of style as audience design is an advance on accommodation theory because it takes more aspects of the speech event into account but it still oversimplifies the situation by trying to make stylistic variation unidimensional. Bell accepts the "universality of a formal-informal continuum subsuming diverse factors" (1984: 181) but the terms "formal" and "informal" are difficult to define precisely and speech events cannot be reduced to this single dimension.

The attempts to quantify stylistic variation have largely been motivated by Labov's preoccupation with linguistic change. While this has clearly led to a greater understanding of the processes of linguistic change, it has not necessarily been beneficial for sociolinguistics as a whole. Since most features of language do not change quickly, if at all (Macaulay, 1988b, 1991a), the concentration on linguistic change in sociolinguistic investigation has probably been counter-productive in some respects. The attempt to obtain quantifiable examples of stylistic variation through the use of written materials has constrained data-collecting unnecessarily. It has also downgraded the notion of style by treating it as unidimensional (Traugott and Romaine, 1985). To adapt Bakhtin's (1981: 263) metaphor the richness of full orchestration has been transposed to a theme played by a penny whistle.

The problem in dealing with style is also methodological. The usual practice in sociolinguistic investigation has been to tabulate tokens extracted from their context and treat them without reference to that context. This

---

[2] On the relationship between the written form and the standard language, see Joseph (1987: 37), Romaine (1989: 577), and Macaulay (1999: 31).

is changing and it is to be hoped that future sociolinguistic studies will pay more attention to the speech events from which the evidence is taken.

In Macaulay (1999) I illustrated how variation between a monophthong and a diphthong in words with the (au) variable among the lower-class speakers in Ayr (Macaulay, 1991a) was affected by a number of factors such as genre and register that could not be reduced to a single stylistic dimension. I also showed how the alternation in negative clitics (–*n't* vs. –*nae*) in the speech of a Dundee woman was affected by the function of the clause (opinion, explanation, or narrative) and also by the social class of the interlocutors in her quoted speech. Such features are easy to identify in Scottish speech because they are quite salient but there is every reason to expect that similar factors may have an effect on variables elsewhere.

In several studies (Macaulay 1991a, 1995, 2005a) I found social class differences in the use of adverbs, but one of my frustrations in looking at this kind of variation was the lack of any kind of comparable data. With rare exceptions (Feagin, 1979; Macafee, 1994) sociolinguists have seldom investigated variation other than phonological or morphological variables, though the situation is changing now. The variation in the use of adverbs in the Ayr and Glasgow materials is style in the sense of Bourdieu's (1991: 38) "different *ways of saying*, distinctive manners of speaking" (emphasis in original). For Bourdieu "what circulates on the linguistic market is not 'language' as such, but rather discourses that are stylistically marked" (1991: 39). This notion of style is the kind that has been investigated, for example, in anthropological studies of the Malagasay (Keenan, 1974), the Ilongot (Rosaldo, 1973), the Quakers (Bauman, 1983), the Wolof (Irvine, 1979, 1990), and the Israeli Sabras (Katriel, 1986). These are studies of 'ways of speaking' (Hymes, 1974) that can be the subject of overt discussion in the community and judged as to their appropriateness in a particular situation. Research on this kind of style, however, tends to be qualitative rather than quantitative and usually carried out through ethnographic methods. Qualitative research alone may provide valuable information about the nature of speech events within a community, but can supply only limited information on the language itself.

What is needed in sociolinguistic investigation is an approach that is flexible enough to analyze samples of speech that can provide a wider range of language use than has generally been the case up till now. Bell's paper at the Stanford workshop (Bell, 2001) argues for a three-layered approach to stylistic analysis:

- Quantification of particular stylistic features
- Qualitative analysis of the individual tokens of stylistic features
- Analysis of the co-occurrence of these features in stretches of language

This is a step in the right direction, but it does not go far enough. What is needed is a broader notion of style that can be employed systematically in sociolinguistic surveys. The advantage of Labov's approach is that it can consistently be employed across a range of interviews. The trade-off is that a major source of variation is deliberately ignored.

The problem with mechanical operational procedures for measuring stylistic variation is that they presuppose that speakers are automata whose behavior can be predicted in terms of external forces, and that cannot be totally true. As Johnstone and Bean point out:

> Class, sex, region, the nature of the linguistic task, and the makeup of the audience all have an important bearing on how people sound; but they do not DETERMINE how people sound.
>
> (Johnstone and Bean, 1997: 236, emphasis in original)

Like so much of what happens elsewhere in linguistics, sociolinguistic studies have tended to concentrate on *form* and ignore function or meaning. How important is this for sociolinguistic investigation? Much will depend upon how successful you believe the field to have been in the past thirty years (Macaulay, 1988b). Like Rickford (1997), in an article examining the 'unequal partnership' between sociolinguistics and the African American speech community, I had at one time thought that sociolinguistic studies would have provided more benefit to the communities in which the research was carried out. In the Glasgow study, I collected a limited amount of information on language use because I was also concerned to investigate attitudes towards Glasgow speech among teachers and employers. It was my hope that the report would prove useful to those involved in the education of children in Glasgow and though it received some attention, I have not heard that it affected the situation significantly. I had expected that there would be many similar studies and that by this date there would have been numerous surveys charting the relationship between language variation and social stratification, but as Rickford comments:

> Contrary to what one might think, the number of full-fledged SOCIAL CLASS studies within sociolinguistics – especially those based on random samples – is rather small, and they date primarily from the 1960's.
>
> (Rickford, 1997: 165)

It would be unfair to attribute this lack solely to the preoccupation with stylistic variation in relation to linguistic change, but trends in research tend to be self-fertilizing. A more comprehensive notion of the variety of language in a community might have provided more useful results for the community. There is no obligation for sociolinguistics to concentrate solely on linguistic change. Stable variation is also worthy of attention.

If Preston (1991, 2001) is correct that stylistic variation reflects social variation and social variation reflects overall linguistic variation, then we need to know more about linguistic variation in the community before attempting to make claims based on stylistic variation. This can be investigated in a variety of ways: (1) by looking at a wider variety of linguistic features (as in Macaulay, 1991a, 2005a, 2005b); (2) by examining the role of all participants in the interaction (as in Bell and Johnson, 1997); (3) by looking at the use of variables in a wide range of contexts (as in Eckert, 2000); (4) by looking at a variety of different speech events (as in Macaulay, 1987a; Johnstone, 1996; Johnstone and Bean, 1997; Coupland, 2001), (5) by looking at the linguistic context in which key variables are used to determine the extent to which they have rhetorical force (as in Eckert, 1996). There is plenty of evidence available, if we are prepared to look beyond the rather narrow focus that has tended to dominate sociolinguistics until now.

Questions for discussion

What is the significance of the difference between weighted and unweighted means?

What are the advantages of developing a scale on which to rank the variants? What are the problems with doing this?

What problems (if any) do you see with Labov's decision to create a style continuum that included spoken and reading examples?

What other speech events are likely to produce the kind of differences shown by Foxy in the McNair-Rickford study?

How important do you consider stylistic differences in studying linguistic variation? Which approach do you favor?

5 Methods of Analysis

The first quantitative studies did not employ any statistical analysis. Labov justified this by drawing attention to the regularity of patterning.

> The fact that this pattern repeats regularly in six different groups, in each style, indicates how pervasive and regular such variable constraints are. We are not dealing here with effects which are so erratic or marginal that statistical tests are required to determine whether or not they might have been produced by chance.
>
> (Labov, 1969: 731)

While this statement may have been valid for Labov's study of the contraction and deletion of the copula, it might not have been so appropriate in his earlier work. As Fasold pointed out:

> Once variability is admitted as a legitimate subject for linguistic analysis, it immediately becomes apparent that methods will be needed to distinguish truly random variability from conditioned variability. It would seem reasonable to turn to the techniques of statistical analysis, which have been designed for just such purposes. But surprisingly, we find no examples of statistical tests having been applied to any of the data in Labov's work, or in the work of Wolfram (1969).
>
> (Fasold, 1972: 33)

Labov's early resistance to statistical analysis certainly made life easier for many of us, but it is legitimate to wonder how many of our claims would have stood up to tests of significance. My Glasgow results received some confirmation from two demonstrations of statistical methods (Berdan, 1978; Cichoki, 1988) using the raw scores for individuals presented in the appendix to the published work (Macaulay, 1977: 162–76). Neither account was designed to test my results but I was pleased to see that their analyses were compatible with what I had found. Berdan demonstrated the use of multidimensional scaling and also principal component analysis. He observed that the weighted index that I had used for the variable (i) gave much the same result as scaling but there was an important difference:

> The weighted index procedure assigns weights to each of the phonetic variants and assumes some ordering among them. The scaling procedure does not make these assumptions. Scaling looks only at the relative differences among the individuals in the use of each of the variants. Despite these differences in assumptions, the two procedures yield virtually identical results.
>
> (Berdan, 1978: 154)

The advantage of multidimensional scaling, however, is that it allows some characterization of the data set without assuming that it is linear. Berdan concludes that it "provides a valuable heuristic tool that makes few assumptions about the nature of the data, but is frequently rather difficult to interpret" (Berdan, 1978: 156).

Cichoki analyzed the same variable from the Glasgow study using Dual Scaling, a multivariate statistical technique. "The technique makes no assumptions about data distributions (such as normality) and is adapted to quantify categorical type data (i.e. categories which cannot be ordered along a continuum" (Cichoki, 1988: 188). His analysis provided a graph demonstrating two dimensions. One reflected the order in my ranking exactly (r. = -0.088). The other dimension distinguished those speakers who had a greater spread of variants from those who used fewer. He pointed out that this kind of information could help the investigator interpret the sociolinguistic situation. Wolfram and Thomas (2002) used linear regression in their examination of age and ethnic differences in Hyde County.

Milroy (1980) employed Analysis of Variance (ANOVA) gender, area, and age differences in the use of five variables and found significant gender differences but only one overall significant difference according to area. An examination of interactions effects showed that the most significant was between gender and age. To investigate the effect of network connections she used Spearman's rank order correlation. This showed an overall correlation between network scores for all five variables but fewer of the detailed comparisons were significant. (The picture is obscured by errors in the reporting of significance in the tables (in the first edition), though the text is clear; the typographical errors were remedied in the second edition (Milroy, 1987).) Bayley (2002: 123–4) points out the disadvantages of ANOVA when there are many factor groups and when there are cells with missing data. Algorithms for calculating ANOVA work best when there are equal numbers in each cell, and that is rarely the case in sociolinguistic studies.

Horvath (1985) introduced a new analytical approach to the study of language variation in her investigation of Australian English. Instead of the correlational methods that had been employed in most earlier studies she used the form of multivariate analysis known as Principal Components Analysis (PCA). She explains that an important characteristic of PCA assumes that all of the variance can be explained by the variables, i.e. it does not resort to any explanation outside of the measured variables. As will be discussed in Chapter 6, this characteristic of PCA may come at a cost.

Horvath comments: "Principal components analysis allows the linguist to study a large number of variables at one time and thereby gain an insight into the *broad* patternings within the speech community" (1985: 178, emphasis added). It is less clear how more detailed information can be extracted from the analysis. (See Chapter 6 for more comments.)

Beginning with Cedergren and Sankoff (1974), the preferred form of multi-variate analysis has been some version of the VARBRUL program, designed specifically to deal with linguistic variation. As Labov observes: "This was a great step forward for the analysis of internal constraints, but not always as helpful when it incorporated social factors" (2006: 402).

There are several good accounts of the program such as Sankoff (1988), Bayley (2002) and Tagliamonte (2006) and I will not attempt to summarize their accounts here. VARBRUL has been extremely successful in dealing with what Bayley (2002: 130–1) calls "properly defined linguistic factors," where inter-action is not a problem. However, social factors often interact and "VARBRUL does not provide a convenient way to test for interaction among factor groups" (Bayley 2002: 130). There are ways of addressing this problem by cross-tabula-tion of factor groups and tracking changes in the factor weights allocated in the step-up/step-down runs of the multivariate analysis (Stephen Levey, p.c.).

Paolillo (2002) points out that few linguistic programs require statistics courses and as a result "variationists find themselves ill-equipped to evaluate competing models of variation" (2002: x). His book has as one of its aims "to bring together as much of the information relevant to variationist methods as can fit comfortably into a single volume" (*ibid.*). Paolillo writes clearly and uses actual data to illustrate different analyses in ways that are very effective.

I have one small quibble about how the results of VARBRUL analyses are sometimes reported. It is common to use the word "constraint" to refer to the factors affecting variation. This is appropriate for phonological factors, since the influence of a following vowel or consonant, for example, has an articula-tory basis. In the case of social factors, however, what the analysis shows are correlations, not constraints. Speakers are not constrained by their social class or gender and the use of the word "constraint" suggests a more deterministic view than is appropriate.

VARBUL requires that the variable be defined in terms of the use or absence of some feature in expressions that are considered to carry the same meaning. In dealing with features that cannot be defined in this way, a different kind of analysis is necessary. In Macaulay (2005a) I compared speakers on the frequency with which they used certain discourse features such as *you know* and *I mean*. The measure I used to test for significance is the Mann-Whitney *U* test (sometimes known as Wilcoxon rank-sum test). This is a non-parametric test for assessing whether two samples of observation come from the same distribution. It requires the two samples to be independent and the observations to be ordinal or continuous measurements. I used the Mann-Whitney to test for age, gender, and social class differences.

Another example of a non-parametric test is CART (Classification and Regression Trees) (Mendoza-Henton, Hay, and Jannedy, 2003: 128–1). Mendoza-Henton et al. point out the advantages of such an approach:

> The construction of classification trees is essentially a type of variable selection. Such trees are a valuable tool for exploratory data analysis and can handle missing values or empty cells with ease, tree construction being based on the cases that do not have missing values. Classification trees are an attractive method of data exploration because they handle interaction between variables automatically. They also have the advantage of being completely nonparametric. No assumptions are made about the underlying distribution of the data. These features make them less powerful for detecting patterns in data, but fairly reliable in terms of the patterns found.
>
> (Mendoza-Henton, Hay, and Jannedy, 2003: 128–9)

It is too early to know how useful this will prove to be as an addition to the statistical analysis of variation.

Variationist studies continue to employ range of statistical measures. As Bayley (2002: 136) observes: "As the field becomes more experienced in quantitative methods, and particularly in the range of available multivariate applications, new creative possibilities for quantitative analysis will doubtless open up." What remains crucial is how to interpret the results.

Question for discussion

What are the advantages and disadvantages of different methods of data analysis?

6 Some Individual Studies

The comments that follow are not intended to provide comprehensive reviews of the works. Instead, they are limited to examining certain methodological procedures and to illustrating the wide variety of methods that investigators have employed. It shows that investigators have been remarkably inventive in the ways they have explored linguistic variation. One of the purposes of considering these works together is to provide a convenient guide to future investigators as to the methodological decisions that have been made in earlier studies. My hope is that this information may make it easier for prospective investigators to avoid re-inventing the wheel or repeating the mistakes of others. For a variety of reasons I have limited the survey to book-length studies of studies dealing with English. Labov (2006) lists thirty-seven studies that followed the example of his New York study (Labov, 1966) more than half of them in languages other than English but generally does not examine the methodology in detail.

William Labov (1966) *The Social Stratification of English in New York City*

Even forty years after its original publication, it is a humbling experience to re-read this work and summarize the many methodological innovations it contains. While Labov was conducting exploratory interviews for the project, he discovered that there had been a comprehensive survey of the Lower East Side by the Mobilization for Youth project and he was able to select a socially stratified sample of native speakers. From a target sample of 195 speakers, he was able to collect interviews from 122 speakers, of which Labov carried out 102, and Michael Kac 20. Of the 73 speakers from the target sample who refused to be interviewed or could not be reached in time to be interviewed fully, Labov was able to elicit information from 33 by the ingenious device of asking questions about television preferences. It is possible that other sociolinguistic surveys have made an equally determined effort to locate and interview refusals, but this is something that is not generally reported. Trudgill (1974) explains why he did not follow up on refusals; in Glasgow (Macaulay, 1977) all the speakers were contacted through the schools and there were no refusals.)

The achievement of personally interviewing 102 speakers is overshadowed by the preparations Labov made for the interview schedule. In addition to developing a questionnaire designed to provide certain information and to elicit certain kinds of speech, Labov prepared a number of test instruments. The most important of these was the Subjective Reaction test in which a tape of five speakers was recorded in which each speaker was heard five times. The first was a neutral passage which contained none of the variables; each of the others focused on one of the variables. Speakers were asked to evaluate the voices in terms of the highest occupation they might occupy. The difference between the ratings for the neutral excerpt and each of the variable excerpts indicated how the interviewees had responded to certain variants on the tape. This is, to my mind, the best example ever of a matched-guise test because the excerpts were from members of the community and chosen to reflect key variables. Too often, though I will not cite examples, the stimulus tape has been blatantly inauthentic. Labov found the perfect way to produce a matched-guise test that was methodologically sound.

I have many reservations, however, about his self-evaluation and linguistic insecurity tests. As I pointed out in an earlier article (Macaulay, 1975), asking questions about the correctness of someone's speech inevitably raises the implication that it might not be 'correct.' In fact, it is reasonable to claim (Macaulay, 1997: 46) that two thirds of Labov's speakers demonstrated a remarkable confidence in their speech and not the linguistic insecurity that Labov interpreted. Nevertheless, Labov's tests were the first attempt to obtain this kind of information.

In addition to the tests, Labov also created two reading passages, one of which focused on the key variables in separate paragraphs and the other including examples of minimal (or near-minimal) pairs in close proximity. He also had a word list of key words, and a list with minimal pairs juxtaposed. Such lists have been used by many subsequent investigators, but it was Labov who first introduced the idea. Labov's use of these written materials to indicate stylistic variation has been discussed in a previous chapter, but the creation of such a complex set of materials for the interviews was a remarkable achievement, and it is important to remember that Labov had no earlier models to follow. He was a true pioneer.

Roger W. Shuy, Walter A. Wolfram and William K. Riley (1968a) *Field Techniques in an Urban Language Study*

This is one of the most remarkable works on sociolinguistics ever published, both for what it contains and for what is missing. Roger Shuy has never struck me as a member of the warrior class but the Detroit Dialect Study was planned like a military operation. The project completed "702 interviews in 31 school districts and over 250 families" (1968a: 10), within a period of ten weeks, employing a team of eleven interviewers. Teams of 2–4 interviewers were sent out by car from the hotel headquarters. "The evening before a given day's work the administrative assistant and the director devised fieldwork teams for the ensuing day based on routing possibilities, fieldworker special-ities, and available drivers" (1968a: 25). We are given information on field-worker orientation, fieldwork (including transcripts of two interviews), and a chapter on fieldwork information. Anyone planning an ambitious commu-nity study would benefit from this account of procedures and problems. There is a great deal of detail on the selection of the sample and the classifica-tion of the speakers into social classes (though it should serve as a cautionary tale rather than as an example to be followed. On the other hand, we are told almost nothing about the survey itself. We do not know the composition of the sample in terms of age, social class or ethnicity. No quantitative informa-tion of any variable is presented. Although Labov, Yaeger, and Steiner (1972) made use of a few speakers from the Detroit Survey, most of the material has lain dormant since 1968. What little we know about the survey comes from Wolfram's (1969) study of a sub-sample of the speakers. The volume was published by the Center for Applied Linguistics, of which Roger Shuy was the director of the sociolinguistics program. Perhaps a different publisher would have requested some editorial changes.

Roger W. Shuy, Walter A. Wolfram and William K. Riley (1968b) *A Study of Social Dialects in Detroit*

The final report to the Office of Education contains much information that was omitted from the published version. The account of the field methods is much the same but there is a great deal of additional material under the headings "Analytical procedures," "Structural frequencies," and "Computer based phonological analysis." There is also a section on "Some sociolinguistic implications for the teaching of English." Under analytical procedures there is an investigation of multiple negation, and pronominal apposition (e.g. *me and my brother we went to the park*). To examine these features a sub-sample of 36 speakers was chosen, half of them children 10–12, and the rest equally divided into older siblings and adults, two-thirds female, and a similar proportion of lower-class speakers, and roughly equal numbers of White and Black speakers. The age, gender, and social class imbalance makes the results of limited interest, but the analysis demonstrates an early approach to the study of grammatical variation. There is an extended analysis of nasalization but the results are inconclusive. The Structural Frequency Study is based on only four speakers and examines the frequency of clause types, coordination, relative clauses, noun phrases, and relative pronouns. I found this interesting because the social class difference anticipates some of my findings in Scotland (Macaulay 1991a, 2005a), but I had not seen the report when I carried out my investigation.

The section on Computer Based Phonological Analysis is enough to make an old man cry. It begins

> After the fieldworkers phonetically transcribed section V of every interview, these transcriptions were recoded into alpha-numeric symbols which were keypunched and verified for a computer retrieval program.
>
> (Part III B, p. 1)

Section V contains at least 120 items. If I understand the report correctly this means that each of these was coded along with "thirty-four fields ... devoted to background information" for all 702 interviews. Few sociolinguists nowadays will even be able to imagine the Herculean task of code-punching such a vast number. I rather hope that I have misunderstood what was done.

The report, which I had not read until recently, makes clear why the published version did not include any results. While the methodology employed in the analysis shows the pioneering spirit of the whole enterprise, the results can only be indicative of questions to investigate further. Like the published version, the report is reticent about the nature of the sample. Given the care with which the whole operation was planned, it is surprising that we are not told more about the distribution of speakers. Nor are we told much about differences that might have arisen in the recordings through the use of a team of interviewers. (We are not told much about the interviewers either, though it is clear that Bill Riley and Walt Wolfram were among the most successful, but we would have guessed that anyway.) I like to think that some day someone will make use of this vast data set and extract some precious information.

William Labov, Paul Cohen, Clarence Robins and John Lewis (1968) *A Study of the Non-standard English of Negro and Puerto Rican Speakers in New York City*, 2 vols

For his second major project, Labov had more economic and human support. The project was supported by the Cooperative Research Program of the

Office of Education, and the Office of Education certainly got their money's worth. Because one of the motivations for the project was to understand some of the difficulties some Black children had in reading, the main target was Central Harlem. Labov had the assistance of three valuable associates, two of whom were African Americans, and they succeeded in interviewing 388 individuals, including approximately a hundred each of pre-adolescent and adolescent boys, a truly heroic number, but that was not the peak of their success. The team organized a series of group sessions, thirty-four in all, in which they had adolescents interacting energetically, eating, drinking, playing cards, watching video-tapes, and arguing in the presence of recording equipment.

Much of the material from the investigation has been reported in Labov (1972b) and various articles, but the original report gives a lot more detail and in particular relates the problems and successes of organizing group sessions with pre-adolescents and adolescents. This is obviously a very good way to get reasonably naturalistic speech from young people, but that does not mean that it is easy. Labov and his associates spent a lot of time planning and preparing the ground to create the best possible setting for spontaneous interaction. Anyone interested in emulating this example would do well to study the report carefully and be prepared to spend considerable time and effort in setting the scene. Quick and easy methods are not likely to work in these situations, and the imaginative and sensitive efforts of Labov and his associates show the kind of commitment needed.

It is a pity that the report has not been commercially published in its entirety because it is a classic and as the authors state "Although only a part of the material available in our records has been analyzed, it is the largest single body ever gathered on systematic and inherent variation within a speech community" (Vol. 1, p. 91). That was certainly true at the time and I believe it still to be true. The first volume deals with phonological and grammatical analysis, the second with the use of language in the speech community. As Labov (2006: 382) points out "The Harlem study was the first to consider internal constraints on linguistic variables, and introduced the notion of the variable rule, in which probabilities were associated with these constraints as well as the social characteristics of the speakers."

The linguistic analysis in Vol.1 employs a form of rule-writing current at the time of writing the report. (It might be rewarding for a young syntactician to re-examine some of this material in terms of a current model of syntactic structure.) The report begins by stating that accurate sociolinguistic analysis depends upon what they call *the principle of accountable reporting*:

A report of a linguistic form or rule used in a speech community must include an account of the total population of utterances from which the observation is drawn, and the proportion of the expected environments in which this form did in fact occur.

(Vol. 1, p. 70)

Consequently, both standard and nonstandard grammatical forms are reported in order to show their relationship:

Sociolinguistic analysis does not consist of simply obtaining more and more precise data on social differentiation or linguistic variation, but rather on showing more clearly the internal and external relations of the elements of the rules, i.e., the factors which govern the use, structure and development of language.

(Vol. 1, p. 81)

This is a noble goal, though personally I would be pleased also to see a few studies that would provide some "more precise data on social differentiation or linguistic variation," even if the analysis did not clearly reveal "the internal and external relations of the elements of the rules."

The first volume examines (t/d) consonant cluster simplification, (s/z) inflections, the contraction and deletion of the copula, the verbal paradigm, negative concord, questions, and other syntactic variables. Consistent with the principle of accountable reporting, there is a rich collection of examples. This project was the first to introduce the notion of network connections. By this means, Labov et al. were able to distinguish gang members from "lames" (those boys who were not fully integrated into the street culture) and show how this status was reflected in their speech. The volume also includes an account of the ingenious memory tests that the team employed to tap into the adolescents' ability to process and repeat certain kinds of sentence.

Complying with the aims of the project, the first volume concludes with "an overview of the relations between NNE (Non-standard Negro English) and SE (Standard English), and some educational implications. The chapter points out the key areas in which differences between NNE and SE are likely to create problems, particularly for reading, and concludes

…a clear understanding of the range of tolerable differences between SE and NNE is essential if there is to be communication between student and teacher, if reading itself is to be taught, and if the sharp stratification of the community is to give way before a strong upward movement which is still missing in the ghetto areas today.

(Vol. 1, 345)

Forty years later, judging by the Oakland School Board Ebonics fiasco (Vaughn-Cooke, 2007), the clear understanding has not yet been reached.

The second volume deals with the use of language in the NNE community and examines such speech events as toasts, sounding, signifying, playing the dozens, and other forms of ritual insults. It also reports the results of a range of correction tests, subjective reaction tests, and a family background test. The volume includes a chapter on narrative analysis that has also been published separately. Like the first volume, this is a rich source of material, some of which has not been published elsewhere. It is probably too late to publish this work in its entirety, but copies should be made available in all libraries where sociolinguistics is taught so that students can consult it. If the original tapes still exist in good condition, there is probably much more that could be extracted from them, especially in terms of discourse features, since this is a potentially rich source of material.

Walt Wolfram (1969) *A Sociolinguistic Description of Detroit Negro Speech*

It is with some embarrassment that I re-read my review of this work in the journal *Language* (Macaulay, 1970), because many of the criticisms I made of Wolfram's study apply equally strongly to my later work (Macaulay, 1977). In particular, I deplored the inadequate treatment of stylistic variation compared with that in Labov (1966). My criticisms were directed as much at the original Detroit Survey (Shuy, Wolfram, and Riley, 1968b) as at Wolfram himself. The sample for Wolfram's volume consisted of 48 speakers 'evenly distributed among four social classes referred to here as upper-middle, lower-middle, upper-working, and lower-working class' (Wolfram, 1969: 15). In each group there were four pre-adolescents, four teenagers, and four adults (30–55 years old), with equal numbers of males and females. Wolfram also had a comparison group of 12 upper-middle-class white speakers, divided similarly by age and sex. All these speakers were chosen from over 700 interviews conducted by the Detroit Dialect Survey. I will not repeat my evaluation here, since it can be found in the review for *Language*, but my main concern was that the Detroit Survey had not been designed to focus on the specific variables that Wolfram was investigating. I did, however, agree that Wolfram had done well in analyzing his materials.

William Labov, Malcah Yaeger and Richard Steiner (1972) *A Quantitative Study of Sound Change in Progress*

Even for someone familiar with the scope of Labov's work it is a humbling experience to return to this work. The investigators report that "we mapped the vowel system of 245 speakers. Approximately 16,000 sections of speech were measured through two to four spectrographic displays" (Vol.1, p. 3). Yet again this represents an unprecedented data set, though the report itself does not deal with all the speakers or all the displays. The report begins with an account of the selection of informants and techniques of interviewing (Vol.1, 16–24). This section contains much useful information on these topics, but its relevance to the main findings is less obvious. For example, the section on the selection of informants stresses the value of getting samples from several members of the same family, but none of the examples of vowel systems in the report deals with members of the same family.

This work represents a complete break with Labov's previous work. In place of perceptually assigned variants, there are charts showing the distribution of locations on diagrams showing "two-formant plots with F1 increasing from top to bottom on the vertical axis, and F2 increasing from right to left on the horizontal axis" (Vol.2, introductory note). There is no grouping of speakers into categories and averaging the results. The evidence is taken from the speech of individuals who are presented (without much supporting evidence) as examples of certain kinds of speakers. We have come a long way from the random sample used in the New York study.

As the title indicates, this is a study of sound change, not an investigation of variation within a single community. In this it anticipates Labov's later volumes on sound change (Labov 1994, 2001). There is a lot of sociolinguistic information in these volumes and many interesting observations on the distribution of variants in different communities, but this information is distributed throughout the two volumes. For anyone interested in the communities Labov investigated, there are some useful observations, though they tend to be scattered throughout the work. From the 16,000 sections of spectrographic displays, 150 diagrams are shown, a proportion that will no doubt strike terror into the hearts of those following in Labov's (yet again) pioneering footsteps.

Peter Trudgill (1974) *The Social Differentiation of English in Norwich*

It is clear even from the title that the model for this work was Labov (1966), though Trudgill takes issue with Labov's condemnation of 'purely descriptive studies' (Labov, 1966: v). This is appropriate since Trudgill was able to make use of Guy Lowman's records of field-work carried out in 1936 for the *Linguistic Atlas of the Eastern United States* and later field-work records for the *Survey of English Dialects*. As I pointed out in my review for *Language* (Macaulay, 1975), future scholars might find it difficult to make use of Trudgill's findings because of the manner in which they are presented. Trudgill followed Labov in distinguishing between formal and casual speech in the interview, and having a reading passage, two word lists, and a minimal pairs list.

Trudgill also followed Labov's example in the use of a linguistic variable to group the speakers into social classes. Trudgill created a social class index based on a six-point scale for five indicators: Occupation, Income, Education, Locality, and Housing, giving equal weight to each category. This provided an index that ranged from 2 to 30 for the sample. In order to group the speakers into social class groups, Trudgill used the frequency with which speakers used third-person singular present tense forms without an inflectional *–s*. Because of the small number of forms provided by some speakers, Trudgill gave the percentage scores for each group in the social class index, but he does not provide the raw figures that would have shown how many tokens were counted. On the basis of these scores he identified five social class groups: Middle middle-class, Lower middle-class, Upper working-class, Middle working-class, and Lower working-class. In keeping with Labov's example, Trudgill does not employ any statistical analysis but most of the graphs that he provides for the variables suggest that the differences between the three working-class groups were probably not significant. This does not undermine his overall findings but neither does it validate his method of identifying social class groups.

Ronald Macaulay (1977) *Language, Social Class, and Education: A Glasgow Study*

This was too ambitious a project right from the start. The original plan was to conduct interviews with three categories of Glaswegians:

   a. A sample of native Glasgow speakers, whose recorded speech was to be described and analyzed.
   b. A sample of Glasgow teachers, whose opinions about language, and the language of their pupils, within the context of education were to be described.
   c. A sample of employers in Glasgow, mainly of personnel managers of firms which recruit in the Glasgow area, whose opinions on language within the context of employment were to be described.

(Macaulay and Trevelyan, 1973: 19)

The community sample was intended to include 10-year-olds, 15-year-olds, university students and young adults not attending university, parents of the 10 and 15-year-olds, and people over fifty. In the end, because of limited time and resources, only the children and their parents were interviewed for the community sample. In just under three months, I interviewed 130 individuals, including teachers and employers. In retrospect, I would probably have made better use of my time if I had completed the community sample instead of interviewing the teachers and employers. While the responses the latter two groups gave were interesting enough, they did not offer any great insights into language variation in Glasgow. In reporting their comments in detail, however, it was my hope that they might be of some use to teachers in the system.

Five phonological variables were chosen for analysis: (i) the vowel in *hit*, (u) the vowel in *school*, (a) the vowel in *hat*, (au) in *now*, and (gs) glottal stops for [t]. Three of these turned out to have problems that were not fully addressed in the analysis. The results for two of them, (u) and (au), are confounded because the tokens extracted did not all come from the same word class. In the case of the (a) variable I excluded all the words in which RP speakers use a back vowel [ɑ:] in words such as *psalm* because for most Scots pronounce it as *Sam*, so the contrast does not exist for them. I excluded the [ɑ:] words because I was worried that some of the middle-class speakers would make a distinction. In this I was wrong, and was severely criticized for this decision.

Despite my criticism of Wolfram (1969) for ignoring stylistic variation, I made no attempt to distinguish styles in the interview itself and was careful not to attach much significance to the differences between speaking and reading aloud. In imitation of Labov (1966) I had prepared a Subjective Evaluation tape, but it was a poor imitation of the original, though it elicited fairly consistent responses to the examples. On looking for a reference in the text some years ago, I was appalled to find that the book has no index.

Crawford Feagin (1979) *Variation and Change in Alabama English: A Sociolinguistic Study of the White Community*

This is the first sociolinguistic study to have as one of its main targets upper-class speakers.[1] Feagin collected information on the speech of 205 individuals but her analysis focuses on 82 whose speech was recorded in interviews. The sample consisted of roughly equal numbers of working-class and upper-class speakers, adults over the age of 65 and teenagers, and both sexes. She also

---

[1] Labov in his introduction refers to a completed study of the upper class by Anthony Kroch but as far as I can tell it had not been published by this time.

interviewed 15 rural, working-class speakers over the age of 65. Feagin gives a detailed account of the social status of her speakers, providing an interesting view of Anniston society. As Labov observes in his introduction to the volume "Feagin's portrait of the class system in Anniston is far more vivid and informative than the skeletal descriptions we have had in the past from sociolinguistic monographs" (1979: xi). The fieldwork covered a period of five years (1968–73) on trips to Anniston. Although Feagin had grown up there, she had left at the age of fifteen, but she was able to return there as "the Youngs' granddaughter" or "Cy and Penny's niece" (1979: 24). Her family connections gave her an access to upper class speakers that might have been difficult (or impossible) for most investigators. On the other hand, she "knew very little about the urban working and lower classes" (1979: 24). Feagin, consequently, is an insider for one part of the fieldwork and an outsider for the other.

Instead of dealing with pronunciation, Feagin concentrates on syntax and morphology: aspect, modality, person-number agreement, and negation. She is able to show significant social class differences in the use of *done* as an auxiliary, the use of double modals, and age differences in the greater use of *get* passives by the teenagers. The most important result of her fieldwork, however, is the wealth of examples given to illustrate the uses of the variables. It is a valuable contribution to dialectology as well as to sociolinguistics.

Lesley Milroy (1980) *Language and Social Networks*

It is somewhat humbling for a mere male to note that the most adventurous, not to say heroic, collectors of sociolinguistic data are all women: Milroy (1980), Cheshire (1982) and Eckert (1989, 2000). Of these, Lesley Milroy was both the pioneer and the one at greatest risk. Given the explosive political situation in Northern Ireland at the time, the Milroys believed that the fieldworker had to be a woman.[2] None of the comments that follow should be interpreted as suggesting anything other than admiration for the magnificent achievement this project represents.

Milroy emphasizes the importance of looking at stylistic variation, but in fact gives only one example (Milroy 1980: 102) where she lists the figures for thirteen Ballymacarett informants for two variables in Spontaneous Style, Interview Style, and Word List Style. The examples of Interview Style are taken from early

---

[2] Those who have witnessed Lesley Milroy in action at professional meetings would have had no anxiety about her ability to defend herself in antagonistic situations.

stages in a formal interview and thus do not fairly represent the kind of speech that can be recorded in an interview. She was probably influenced by Wolfson (1976) who presents a similar negative view of interviews, but this has subsequently been contradicted by many examples where fluent, spontaneous speech has been recorded in interviews (Macaulay, 1984, 1991a, 2005b; Schiffrin 1987; Rickford and McNair, 1994). The figures from the Word List and Milroy's comments show the difficulty of contrasting reading with speaking. Apart from this one example Milroy concentrates only on Spontaneous Style, namely the free conversation recorded informally in sessions in the speakers' homes. Judging from the illustrations in Milroy and Milroy (1977) the quality of speech recorded is obviously very good and one can only regret that Milroy did not choose to investigate more than the nine phonological variables.

   Instead of stylistic differences Milroy focuses on gender differences and differences between the three communities she studied, Ballymacarrett, Clonard, and Hammer, and following the example of Labov et al. (1968) showed the importance of network connections in accounting for differences in the use of the variables. In her first chapter Milroy observes "we still know very little about the *total* linguistic repertoires of individuals or communities" (1980: 1, emphasis in original), but in fact her study shows very little of the complex sociolinguistic situation in Belfast since it is limited to three small working-class communities. Milroy, however, was a pioneer in another way being the one of the first sociolinguists to introduce measures of statistical significance in her analysis. From this time onwards it would no longer be possible for sociolinguists to present figures with no indication of their statistical validity.[3]

Jenny Cheshire (1982) *Variation in an English Dialect: A Sociolinguistic Study*

Cheshire's study was the first sociolinguistic study of nonstandard grammar in the speech of English adolescents. She collected her data by an arduous method. She visited two adventure playgrounds in Reading, England and made friends with a group of nine boys at one playground, and a group of eleven girls at the other, plus three boys at the second location. "Both playgrounds were visited two three times a week for a period of nine months" (1982: 14–15). Even those who have not suffered the rigors of the English climate will recognize what a heroic effort this must have been. "The total data

---

[3] Readers of the first edition should note that Tables 6.3 and 6.4 contain errors in the representation of significant results. This is because the symbol "<" occurs for all the entries in the column headed 'level of significance' when in 16 cases it should have been ">" indicating that the results were not significant, as the text makes clear. These errors are corrected in the second edition (Milroy 1987).

used as the basis for analysis amounted to eighteen hours of speech" (1982: 19). Assuming (at a minimum) 180 hours spent at the playgrounds, this is a poor return in terms of quantity but the benefit is in terms of the quality of speech recorded. Cheshire illustrates this with excerpts from sessions recorded in school with teachers where the kind of speech is markedly different.

The age range of the speakers is 11 to 17 for the boys and 9 to13 for the girls. Cheshire comments: "Although there is a difference in the ages of male and female speakers a statistical analysis of variance showed that this difference is not significant" (1982: 22). With this small number there is no way the differences could be statistically significant, but that is irrelevant to Cheshire's concerns. The girls are younger than all but four of the boys. That could be significant. Cheshire also claims that according to the occupation of the parents "the children can be considered as forming a relatively homogeneous social group" (1982: 25). This is probably accurate since most of the parents have similar occupations, but there are two anomalies in the parents of the girls. Two fathers of the girls are reported to work as chefs, a description that seems a notch up from painter or brick layer, and it may not be a coincidence that the mothers in each case are reported to be 'housewife.' All the other mothers have been reported to be employed, the majority as 'cleaner.' There are suggestions of a social class difference there.

Cheshire identified 14 morphological and syntactic features that have nonstandard variants in her recordings. She developed an index for each speaker of the number of times that speaker used the nonstandard form as a percentage of the total number of times that the form was used, either the standard or nonstandard variety. Although she calculated frequency indices for individual speakers, she used group indices in her comparisons "in order to eliminate bias in cases where some speakers use a feature only rarely" (1982: 28). This is, of course, a perennial problem when dealing with other than frequently occurring phonological and morphological features. The low threshold is indicated by the fact that "any figures arising from fewer than five occurrences are given in parentheses" (1982: 28). Cheshire's decision to present her results only as percentages is not unique, but it is unfortunate in terms of full disclosure. There is no way to tell from a percentage how many examples are included. Cheshire does not generally give raw figures but in a rare exception she cites the number of tokens for Tables 12 and 13 of Chapter 4. In these tables she is comparing older speakers and younger speakers and there are 12 percentages given, but for Table 12 she gives the number of tokens as 27 and for Table 13 as 23. There may be some error in the reporting here but it is hard to take seriously the reporting of percentages when the average number of tokens per cell is only two. Most of Cheshire's figures, of course, will have larger numbers, but the failure to report the actual figures leaves the percentages suspect.

Cheshire follows Milroy (1980) and anticipates Eckert (1989, 2000) and Fought (1997) in providing an ethnographic account of the relations among the teenagers. This suggests explanations for the different percentages of the variables that have been presented earlier. There is much of interest in this narrative account but from a variationist perspective its value is limited because of the manner in which the figures for the variation have been reported. Despite these limitations, Cheshire's study remains a pioneering effort in the investigation of teenage speech.

Barbara Horvath (1985) *Variation in Australian English*

Horvath (1985) introduced a new analytical approach to the study of language variation. Instead of the correlational methods that had been employed in earlier studies she used the form of multivariate analysis known as Principal Components Analysis (PCA). She explains an important characteristic of PCA:

> Principal components analysis is very similar to factor analysis except that the latter assumes a general factor to explain part of the variance whereas the former assumes that all of the variance can be explained by the variables, i.e., it does not resort to any explanation outside of the measured variables.
>
> (Horvath, 1985: 53)

Horvath and her team interviewed 177 speakers (out of a planned sample of 180) in 1979 and 1980. The sample was chosen to give a balanced representation of three social class groups with equal numbers of adults and teenagers and equal numbers of males and females from three ethnic groups: Anglos, Italians, and Greeks. No attempt was made to restrict the sample to those who were native speakers of English.

Horvath chose five vowel variables and classified the variants as Cultivated, General, Broad, and Ethnic Broad, the first three being labels applied by earlier investigators of Australian English (Mitchell and Delbridge, 1965a, b). Thus for each of the vowel variables there were three variants according to a perceived identification with a style of speech. The Ethnic Broad category does not play a major role in the analysis, but a category of Accented was added to refer to those whose English was noticeably different from that of native speakers. The variants for each speaker were entered with the labels A (accented), C (cultivated), G (general), B (broad) and EB (ethnic broad). In contrast to the method employed by Labov (1966), the variants were not totaled and averaged but entered as discrete elements. The first run of the PCA revealed a major split in the sample into what Horvath calls the core speech community and a peripheral speech community. There are 47 speakers in the peripheral group, all adults of either Italian or Greek background, who presumably fell into the category of Accented. The peripheral speakers were excluded from further analysis, which dealt only with the speakers in the core. This decision destroyed the age and ethnic balance in the sample because there are 90 teenagers and only 40 adults. More importantly, perhaps, all but 10 of the ethnic speakers are teenagers, so 75 percent of the adult speakers in the core community are Anglo.

Horvath argues in favor of a PCA approach: "Perhaps the most attractive reason for choosing a method that allows grouping of speakers according to their linguistic behaviour rather than according to their place in a social grid is that as linguists it is the linguistic categories that we are most concerned about and most knowledgeable about" (Horvath, 1985: 65–6). I have argued elsewhere against attempts to conduct sociolinguistic investigations on the basis of linguistically determined groups (Macaulay, 1978) because we all belong to 'communities of practice' according to our interests and experience. Bridge players, wine connoisseurs, and devotees of cricket all have a knowledge of language that is not shared by others with different interests, but that does not necessarily make such groupings profitable to study sociolinguistically. The problem with producing linguistically determined groups is that the significance of such groups remains to be identified. For the core speech community PCA revealed that the speakers ranged from -4 to +5 on Principal Component 2. On the basis of this information, Horvath identified four core sociolects, though she does not explain the criteria for separating the groups. From the visual display it is not easy to see why the lines were drawn where they were, though no doubt Horvath had reasons for the decision. In the interests of full disclosure, it would have been helpful to have some explanation of how the division was made.

The numbers in the sociolects vary greatly, from 58 speakers in Sociolect 2 to 8 speakers in Sociolect 4. Sociolect 4 consists of those speakers who use predominantly Cultivated variants, and not surprisingly is 60 percent middle-class. Perhaps less expectedly nearly 50 percent are Greek. Adults make up 60 percent of the group which is also 100 percent female. Horvath does not explore the significance of this group further, which is a pity because it would have been interesting to know how many of the 19 males in Sociolect 3 came close to the females in Sociolect 4. Horvath's analysis remains at a very abstract level and there is little possibility of reconfiguring her results in the way that she was able to demonstrate in her reanalysis of Labov's (1966) data on the variable (dh) (Horvath, 1985: 65).

Horvath ran a separate PCA analysis for four consonantal variables and the use of High Rising Tone (HRT) and she divided the second grid into six sociolects, of which Sociolect D4 corresponds to Sociolect 4 in having eight females, nearly two-thirds are middle-class, half are Greek. A new sociolect is Sociolect D6 which consists of seven Anglo female adults from the lower-working-class and one male, presumably also working-class. There is a larger group, Sociolect D1, which is predominantly Anglo, male, and teenager, spread across all three social class categories.

The picture that emerges from Horvath's study is that there is a regression to the mean, with fewer speakers employing either Broad or Cultivated variants. This is what one might expect in a country that has probably become less rigidly stratified since the end of World War II. The Cultivated form of speech was obviously based on British models, while the Broad variety was a revolt against such a standard. With the British influence waning and being replaced by an American one, it is hardly surprising that the General variants should dominate the scene.

As Horvath points out in her concluding remarks: "Principal components analysis allows the linguist to study a large number of variables at one time and thereby gain an insight into the broad patterning within the speech community" (1985: 178). Horvath certainly succeeded in demonstrating the use of the technique and illustrating the kinds of conclusions that can be reached from the results. Why, then, do I find myself feeling frustrated with the work? Partly, it is because Horvath chose to ignore the kinds of questions that usually interest sociolinguists: Which specific variables differ between male teenagers and female teenagers? Which specific variables differ between Anglo adults and Anglo teenagers? Which specific variables are used differentially by the three social class groups? Since each of these categories has an equal number of speakers, the correlations would have been easy to make. It would also have been possible to make direct comparisons between Anglo teenagers, Greek teenagers, and Italian teenagers in terms of the individual variables. There also could have been more direct examination of gender differences. Horvath deals with these questions at some distance. I would have preferred more investigation of these questions in a form that would allow for comparison with other studies of language variation.

I also wish Horvath had been more curious about the distribution of the variables. For example, is there anything special about the eight females in Sociolect 4 who use mainly Cultivated variants? How many of them went to private schools (a major influence on speech at one time)? What about the seven lower-working-class Anglo women in Sociolect D6? Was there anything in common that made them into a group that is distinct from Anglo working-class men and Anglo working-class teenagers? I also wonder to what extent the results were influenced by the speech of the interviewers. Were any of them Cultivated speakers? This is probably too difficult a question to answer, but one wonders.

Horvath collected a rich data base (despite the unbalanced sample) and I feel that she has left too much of it unmined. The clarity with which she presents her results will provide a valuable example for anyone wishing to employ this approach. Nobody will be surprised that I would not recommend such a course, but Horvath has shown how it can be done.

Nikolas Coupland (1988) *Dialect in Use: Sociolinguistic Variation in Cardiff English*

Coupland employed an ingenious approach to overcome the Observer's Paradox. He recruited an assistant in a travel agency in Cardiff to allow recording of her interactions with clients. Fifty-one clients were recorded and later asked for their permission to use the recordings and also some information about themselves. (There were an additional four who refused permission.) On the basis of the background information, the clients were assigned to three social classes: Professional and Intermediate, Skilled non-manual, Skilled manual and Unskilled. The recordings were searched for tokens of five consonantal variables.

   Coupland calculated percentages of the use of the nonstandard variants for each speaker and then calculated the mean of the percentages for each occupation and education group, but he omitted from the calculations any cases where the speaker had fewer than four instances of the variable. As a result, his findings are based on the speech of, at most, 34 individuals in the case of the (h) variable to only 28 in the case of intervocalic (t). Thus a small sample was reduced even further, but Coupland was able to demonstrate consistent patterns of variation according to occupation, education, and gender, though he points out that the mean deviations were high "showing that there is as much variation between individuals within some of socioeconomic groups as there is between the most representative members of adjacent groups" (1988: 92). This was an original approach to the study of variation and it is perhaps surprising that others have not followed Coupland's example and explored similar kinds of situations. In addition to the information on the clients, Coupland was also able to show the effect of addressee and context on the speech of the assistant.

Ronald Macaulay (1991a) *Locating Dialect in Discourse: The Language of Honest Men and Bonnie Lasses in Ayr*

This volume is a phoenix that rose out of the ashes of a failed project. After investigating language variation in Glasgow (Macaulay, 1977), it struck me that there would be value in exploring to what extent the kind of variation found in Glasgow might be reproduced (or not) in other urban communities in Scotland. With a population of around five million, it seemed to me that the entire country could be conceived of as a single speech community. Certainly, there is no denying that the vast majority of the population distinguish themselves from their southern neighbors by the way in which they speak. This was confirmed for me by the consistent response to the question *What do you think marks the biggest difference between the Scots and the English?* which was always "the way we speak."

To explore this possibility I interviewed 10-year-olds, 15-year-olds, and adults in Aberdeen, Ayr, and Dundee. (I did not include Edinburgh because there was an ongoing study into linguistic variation there.) My obstinate persistence in proceeding with the project in the face of limited success resulted in a large number of unusable recordings. The biggest failure was with the 15-year-olds. In Glasgow I felt that I had done reasonably well with this age group but for some reason I was not able to reproduce this result elsewhere. (I still have a stack of these tapes to remind me of this ego-undermining experience, but I have no desire to listen to them.) I was somewhat more successful with the 10-year-olds, particularly the girls, and I succeeded in recording a number of jump-rope and other rhymes that had not been published before (Macaulay, 2006a: 182–91). I had mixed success with the adults but I was able to use some of these materials in a volume about uses of language (Macaulay, 2005b). The original plan, however, increasingly began to seem unrealistic, and circumstances prevented me from proceeding further with it.

An administrative appointment beginning in 1980 restrained me from conducting more interviews for this project, so I decided to make use of some of the materials I felt comfortable about using. There were twelve interviews with adults in Ayr, with equal numbers of middle-class and lower-class, though unfortunately there were only three women in the sample. Contrary to earlier work on language variation I chose to transcribe these interviews in their entirety and store them on a computer. I then went through each interview and coded the lines in terms of 49 different syntactic categories. This allowed me to investigate possible social class differences in syntax.

In addition to clear phonological and morphological differences, I was able to show social class differences in seven types of syntactic constructions. I did not, however, test for statistical significance and some of the differences were slight. (The raw figures are given in an appendix, so they are available to anyone interested in submitting them to a test.)

Penelope Eckert (2000) *Linguistic Variation as Social Practice: The Linguistic Construction of Identity in Belten High*

This is, and will no doubt continue to be, the classic example of combining ethnographic and quantitative methods in sociolinguistics. Eckert spent more than two years observing the high school community and recording interviews. From a total of 200 interviews, she selected 69 for analysis, and for comparison she and a colleague interviewed 20 students at each of three high schools in neighboring communities. The interviews provide the data for the quantitative measures but the depth in the analysis comes from Eckert's immersion in the daily life of the students over the two years of the study. She did not interview anyone until she had got to know that person quite well and could therefore carry on a comfortable conversation with her or him. The "interviews" consequently do not suffer from the kind of awkwardness sometimes attributed to 'interview style' (Milroy and Milroy, 1977; Wolfson, 1976).

Eckert analyzed nine vocalic variables and one grammatical variable (negative concord). For each speaker, 50 tokens of each variable were identified by a systematic process from the transcript of the entire interview. All the variables were coded for a range of possible internal constraints:

preceding and following segment
emphatic length and stress
preceding and following (where applicable) word boundary
occurrence in open vs. closed syllable
stress: primary, secondary, or monosyllable
common vs. proper noun
lexical item in which the token occurs

(Eckert, 2000: 88)

Then a Varbrul iterative process searched for "the best fit between linguistic variables and the internal constraints on their form on the one hand, and the social phenomena under examination on the other" (2000: 88). For each of the vocalic variables, Eckert lists the percentage of each variant in the corpus and the ranking of the internal constraints. This provides a solid basis for the examination of social factors that affect the use of particular variants. It also provides a model for future studies of this kind.

Although Eckert's study is most frequently cited with reference to the "communities of practice" represented by the Jocks and the Burnouts, Eckert does not ignore the larger social context in which the adolescents live. As Eckert herself points elsewhere "ethnographic studies cannot transcend the local unless they have a broader structure to orient to" (Eckert, 2003: 116). Accordingly, she created socioeconomic indices for the parents, based on education, occupation, and residence. Negative concord was the variable that showed the strongest correlation with parents' education. Only one of the vocalic variables (ay) showed any correlation with educational level and that was for the parents of girls. Eckert suggests that the absence of correlation with the parents' socioeconomic indices could be a consequence of the sampling method, which was not designed to represent a comprehensive socioeconomic sample. However, Eckert also points out that this lack of evidence from the parents does not weaken "the heart of this research, which focuses on the nature of adolescence, and particularly on the relation between the speaker's construction of identity and linguistic variation" (Eckert, 2000: 111). Anyone planning a study that combines ethnographic and quantitative methods should examine this work very closely. It will repay the effort. My only regret is that Eckert is not more interested in the discourse aspects of speech. Her interviews no doubt contain many features that would be interesting to explore in detail.

Matthew J. Gordon (2001) *Small-town Values and Big-city Vowels: A Study of the Northern Cities Shift in Michigan*

Gordon set out to investigate the spread of the Northern Cities Shift (NCS) in Michigan. He chose two small towns, Paw Paw (pop. 110,000) and Chelsea (pop. 80,000) and interviewed eight males and eight females from each community, half of them adults and half adolescents. They were roughly from the same social background and all European Americans. He recruited them by an informal method and eliminated those clubs and interviews that were unsatisfactory for one reason or another. This is an example that might profitably be followed, though with caution. There is no reason to include in a survey examples that are obviously different speech events (Macaulay, 2001b) unless the motivation is to examine the effect of different conditions. Investigators seldom comment on the quality of their recorded samples though this information might be relevant to the validity of the results.

   Gordon examined six phonological variables by auditory methods, though he carried out one instrumental analysis of each to display the range of variation. For each variable he observed the effect of the voicing, manner, and place of articulation for the consonants preceding and following the vowel, and calculated the chi-square statistical significance of such categories. He also investigated the effect of word length and syllable structure on the variables. He provides the raw numbers as well as the percentages, so his figures could be used for other kinds of analysis. Despite the strictures of Thomas (2002: 169) against impressionistic judgments (see Chapter 2), Gordon's contextual analysis is very impressive. I am unqualified to say whether it will be useful to those studying the Northern Cities Shift.

McCafferty, Kevin (2001) *Ethnicity and Language Change: English in (London) Derry, Northern Ireland*

McCafferty's study is focused on the social aspects of language variation, mainly the ethnic difference between Catholics and Protestants. Having been brought up a Catholic in the city, McCafferty points out that "large areas of the Protestant culture, even of my own home town, have always been largely closed to me" (2001: 14). This made fieldwork problematic in many ways. He describes in detail the ways in which he made contact with potential interviewees at clubs and community centers, establishing some kind of relationship with them before asking them to grant interviews. Given the uncertain political and security situation at the time of his project (1994–95), McCafferty steered clear of direct questions about ethnic differences or loyalties. This is a good account of the problems of collecting suitable recordings in an ethnically divided community. This fieldwork provided a great deal of social information and much of the book is devoted to an ethnographic account of how the situation in (London)Derry affected members of both ethnic groups.

McCafferty collected a total of 187 interviews, of which 107 were suitable for sociolinguistic analysis. This provided a roughly balanced sample of Catholics and Protestants, males and females, middle-class and working-class, teenagers and adults (ages 44–73). McCafferty provides quantitative analysis for six phonological variables. For two of them, the differences among the social categories are so small that the claim of statistical significance (based on chi-square) is irrelevant. He did find, however, for one variable (the FACE vowel) that there was a clear difference between Protestants and Catholics. The innovative form is a diphthong and it is more frequent among Protestants, particularly the middle-class speakers. He claims that this is the first clearly established case of ethnic differences in Ulster. Three other variables show some interesting patterns but this is the most striking finding. Readers, however, should note that McCafferty sometimes changes the presentation of information between the tables, in which the percentages are the proportion of three variants (including the standard form), and the figures where the percentages are of the two nonstandard variants only. The figures, consequently, are not simply a graphic display of the tables.

Anna-Brita Stenström, Gisle Andersen, and Ingrid Kristine Hasund (2002) *Trends in TeenageTalk: Corpus Compilation, Analysis and Findings*

In any empirical investigation, there will be trade-offs. An approach that offers certain benefits usually has limitations in other respects. The method employed by Stenström, Andersen, and Hasund (2002) in collecting data for the Bergen Corpus of London Teenage Language (COLT) illustrates this point. Their aim was to investigate "the London teenage vernacular" (p. 3). They recruited 32 teenagers, aged 13–17, provided them with a Sony Walkman Professional tape recorder and instructed them "to carry this equipment for three to five days and record all the conversations they were engaged in, in as many different situations as possible, preferably with friends of their own age and, if possible, without any of the co-speakers noticing that they were being recorded" (p. 3). The teenagers were recruited from five school boroughs in London and one boarding school in Hertfordshire.

Stenström et al. also assigned the recruits to three social categories, 'high,' 'middle' and 'low' on the basis of "residential borough, parents' occupation and whether the parents are employed or not" (p. 21). However, since "only recruits and their families are classified, only about 50 per cent of the corpus material can be assigned a social group value" (p. 21). In their analysis Stenström et al. make little use of the social categories, preferring to deal with social class differences through the residential characteristics of the boroughs.

The intent of this method was clearly to collect as natural a sample of teenage speech as possible, but as Wolfson (1976) observed 'natural' is a complex notion in language. Stenström et al. point out many of the problems they encountered. Some of the teenagers recorded very little speech and often the quality of the recording was poor. The amount of speech recorded by each participant varied greatly. Two teenagers, a white middle-class boy and a working-class West Indian girl, were each responsible for a tenth of the total amount of speech transcribed for the corpus. Two participants provided no usable samples of speech. The situations in which the recordings were made also differed greatly. Some of the teenagers mainly recorded interactions at home or in class, and one with adults in his father's pub. The largest part of the corpus (61 percent) was recorded by those in middle adolescence (14–16), followed by those in early adolescence (10–13) with 24 percent and those in late adolescence (17–19) with 9 percent. Although the corpus includes samples from 21 boys and only 9 girls, the recordings made by the girls provided 44 percent of the corpus.

Judging from the extracts given in Stenström et al. (2002), the project succeeded in its aim of recording some excellent samples of teenage talk. These provided the basis for an interesting qualitative analysis of the content of the tapes (pp. 27–61). The corpus also supplies a great deal of useful information on the use of slang, swear words, and 'vague words' (pp. 67–106), reported speech (pp. 108–29), non-standard grammar and "the trendy use of intensifiers" (pp. 131–63), the use of tags (pp. 165–91), and 'ritual conflict' (193–209). These materials will provide a basis for comparison for other studies of language variation.

However, Stenström et al. also present some statistical comparisons that are more questionable. For example, they have three tables showing the relationships between slang and gender, slang and age, and slang and school borough (pp. 73–5). Unfortunately, Stenström et al. in their analysis do not show the interdependence of these three variables in their tables. For example, their figures show that males use more slang words than females (p. 73) and also that slang words are used more frequently in the borough of Tower Hamlets (p. 75), but all the recruits in Tower Hamlets are boys (p. 24) and most of their interlocutors would be boys (p. 6). Thus these two findings are closely related.

There are also problems with the size of cells. For example, Stenström et al. show that boys aged 10–13 use slang words much more frequently than girls of the same age. However, in the sample for this age group there are 10 boys (from all social class groups) and only 2 girls, neither in the 'low' social class category. In contrast, among the 17–19 age group, where the girls are shown to be much more frequent users of slang than the boys, in the list of recruits (p. 24) there is only one 17-year-old boy and one 17-year-old girl, both in the 'high' social class category. There is no record of how many interlocutors either had but there is an obvious danger in extrapolating from such a limited sample.

There is perhaps a more fundamental problem with the methodology. Given the instructions the recruits received, there is no control over the kinds of speech events recorded. Since the nature of the speech event will affect the kind of speech recorded (Hymes, 1974), there is no guarantee that the samples of speech can be compared in a systematic way unless they consist of similar speech events (Macaulay, 2001b). The problem is clearly illustrated by those teenagers who chose to record classroom interactions where the principal speaker was the teacher (p. 5) and where the speech of the teenagers would be constrained by the situation. Similarly, some chose to record interactions with their parents and these samples would probably differ from the ways in which they spoke with their peers.

Equally important is the way in which the recruits approached the problem of recording their peers. Fortunately, from an ethical perspective, the recruits apparently did not indulge in much surreptitious recording, despite the instruction from the investigators, but their efforts to get their peers to record interesting speech may sometimes have distorted the situation. For example, as pointed out in Chapter Three, there are indications that some of the recruits actively encouraged their interlocutors to swear on tape (pp. 77–86) and to get into arguments (p. 202) This raises doubts about how useful the results for understanding how the teenagers interact under normal circumstances.

Stenström et al. have provided a valuable glimpse of teenage talk in London but their approach did not solve the problem of recording a suitable sample of speech for comparative statistical analysis.

Ronald Macaulay (2005a) *Talk That Counts: Age, Gender and Social Class Differences in Discourse*

Despite the awkwardness of implying self-praise, I believe that this work exemplifies a kind of cooperation that might be followed in other investigations. In 1997 Jane Stuart-Smith collected samples of Glasgow speech for an investigation of accent and voice quality (Stuart-Smith, 1999), using the methodology employed in an earlier study of Newcastle/Derby speech (Docherty, Foulkes, Milroy, Milroy and Walshaw, 1997). Speakers who were acquainted with each other were recorded in same-sex conversations with no investigator present:

> Thirty-two speakers were recorded, with equal numbers of males and females, adults (40–60 years) and children (13–14 years), from two broadly different social and regional backgrounds of the Glaswegian conurbation: Maryhill, a working-class inner-city area stretching from the north-west of the city centre, and Bearsden, a leafy suburb further out to the north-west, inhabited mainly by the middle-classes.
>
> (Stuart-Smith, 1999: 204)

When I visited Jane Stuart-Smith, she allowed me to listen to extracts from the recordings. I was immediately impressed by the liveliness of the conversations, particularly those of the adolescents. In my own recordings I had sometimes enjoyed equally lively conversations with adults (Macaulay, 1991a) but I had never succeeded in getting anything similar from adolescents. I asked if I could have transcripts and copies of the tapes to investigate discourse features and Jane Stuart-Smith agreed to supply them. This is a rare (perhaps unique) example of a researcher being willing to allow someone else to work on her data before she had completed her project. Whatever value others may grant to my analysis of these features, I believe that this example of scholarly cooperation could be followed by others. There is no reason for those who are primarily interested in phonological or morphological features to expend the time and energy looking at discourse features, but it is unfortunate when valuable samples of speech are allowed to languish unexamined for syntactic, lexical, and other variation.

As in all sociolinguistic analysis there is a great deal of tedium in looking for examples of variation in discourse. The first task was to separate the contribution of each speaker since the transcripts consisted of dialogues. I did this by deleting the contribution of one speaker from the file and saving it as a separate file, then repeating the process for the second speaker. There is probably a way this could have been done by writing a program to do this, but I did it manually. In the process, I learned much about the conversations, some of which proved useful in identifying items to investigate.

The separated files were entered into the WordSmith Program as text-only files and a concordance prepared for each speaker. This provides a total word count and allows individual items to be extracted and counted. For items that have a unique orthographic form, this is a very simple process, but many forms are ambiguous and thus require an examination of the context in which they occur. Fortunately, the WordSmith concordance program supplies enough of this context to separate out the different meanings or functions.

The measure chosen to reflect variation was the frequency for 1,000 words. Since the transcripts provided a word count for each speaker, calculation of these frequencies was a simple matter. The raw figures and calculated frequencies for all the variables for each speaker are displayed in the Appendix (pp. 191–201) so readers can explore other comparisons than those presented in the text. Since the frequencies themselves may give a misleading impression, all the main comparisons were subjected statistical analysis. The statistical measure employed was the Mann-Whitney nonparametric test, considered one of the most powerful nonparametric tests, suitable for data of this kind. The version used was that in SPSS.

Conclusion

The above accounts cover only a fraction of the quantitative investigation of language variation that has been carried out in the past forty years but they show how productive this approach has been. It is clear that sociolinguists have succeeded in recording a large amount of speech that is valuable for plotting the range of variation in many different kinds of community. At the same time, investigators (for obvious reasons) have tended to concentrate on only a small number of features. It seems unfortunate that so much valuable information should languish unexplored in the archives of the investigators.

An encouraging example, however, is set by the Newcastle Electronic Corpus of Tyneside English (NECTE), which has rescued 89 surviving recordings from the 1969 Tyneside Linguistic Survey and made them available online along with 18 recordings from the 1994 Phonological Variation and Change in Contemporary Spoken British English project. It would be very helpful if more investigators were to follow this example, though the cost may often be prohibitive.

Question for discussion

Which project would you choose as a model for future research? Why did you choose this one?

---

7 An Example of Discourse Variation

The previous chapters have examined the methodology employed in various studies of language variation, with the emphasis on the ways in which the evidence has been collected and analyzed. The present chapter illustrates the use of quantitative methods in an investigation of variation in the use of discourse features. It also examines in detail the situational and social factors that can affect the quality of speech recorded.

It goes without saying that any comparison of speakers should be based on speech samples recorded in sufficiently similar circumstances, so that meaningful conclusions can be drawn. Moreover, the samples must come from similar speech events (Macaulay, 2001b). Reading aloud from word lists is one example where comparables samples can be successfully collected, provided the speakers are equally literate (and cooperative). However, only a limited amount of information can be elicited in this way and it may not accurately reflect the speaker's normal practice (Milroy, 1980). If the sociolinguistic investigation is to go beyond phonological and morphological features, substantial amounts of coherent speech will be requited (Macaulay, 1991a). It is, however, not only the amount of speech that is critical but also its quality. The complex factors influencing language use were outlined by Hymes (1974). They include participant role, situation, speech event, style, and genre, and his outline can be helpful in establishing the quality of language recorded.

The present chapter presents the results of a study that employed the technique for collecting speech samples (mentioned in Chapter 3) that was developed by Docherty, Foulkes, Milroy, Milroy, and Walshaw (1997) in which two participants, who know each other, talk together for about half an hour in the presence of a tape-recorder without the investigator present. An examination of a set of examples of speech recorded under these circumstances illustrates the relevance of the factors that Hymes (1974) lists for claims that the samples are appropriate for comparison.

In 2003 Jane Stuart-Smith recorded 36 Glasgow working-class adolescents in same-sex dyads talking to each other for approximately half an hour, with no investigator present, with equal numbers of girls and boys 10–11 years-old, 12–13 years old, and 14–15 years-old.[1] These recordings were part of a complex investigation into the influence of mass media on the speech of working-class Glasgow adolescents. At a later stage in the project, the adolescents were to take part in a mock TV quiz show and this proved to be a powerful motivator.

In 1997 Stuart-Smith had recorded a similar sample of eight middle-class and eight working-class Glasgow adolescents aged 13–14, and a similar number of adults, as part of an investigation into language change (Stuart-Smith, 1999), and these materials provided the basis for an examination of discourse variation (Macaulay, 2005a). In 2004 the two younger groups from 2003 were recorded again under similar circumstances. (The oldest group had mostly left the school by this time and could not be recorded again.)

The recordings were transcribed in their entirety and from each transcript a concordance was created by use of the WordSmith program. These concordances were then combined to provide information on the use of certain features by age and gender categories as well as for the sample as a whole. The results will be examined later but first the quality of the recordings will be examined in terms of the factors in Hymes' (1974) model: Setting, Scene, Participants, Ends, Message form, Key, Instrumentalities, Norms, and Genre.

Setting

The first of Hymes' factors to be considered is the Setting, that is, the physical circumstances, including the time and place of the speech event. For the participants in all three sets of recordings the setting was the same, and the length of the session was just over half an hour. The setting was a room in the school used by teachers and staff as an office. The physical location of the participants facing each other across a table was the same for each pair. There were books and magazines provided, and the participants occasionally commented on them, usually in derogatory terms.

Scene

The next factor given by Hymes is the Scene, that is, the subjective definition of the occasion. All the participants knew that they were being recorded in connection with an investigation into language use. There are various

[1]The project in which the recordings were made was supported by ESRC grant no. R000239757. I am deeply indebted to Jane Stuart-Smith for providing the transcripts and allowing me to make use of them for this chapter. The sessions were arranged and conducted by the research assistant on the project Claire Timmins. It is clear from the transcripts that part

comments that reflect this awareness. In other words, the participants knew what kind of speech event they were participating in.

There are often references to the difficulty of finding something to talk about. In all the sessions there are references to the recording situation. Some of the participants commented on the recording levels, experimenting with different ways of affecting the volume, including detaching themselves from the microphone briefly to move. They are very interested in how much time there is left, particularly towards the end of the session. The adolescents are fully aware that they are being recorded and they know that they are expected to talk to each other. They sometimes berate their partner for not saying enough.

Participants

Hymes' third factor concerns the Participants. In each session the adolescents were of similar age, gender, and social class background. There were consequently no external factors of these kinds that would have affected role relationships in the interaction. Obviously, there were personal differences between the pairs of interlocutors but these did not prevent sustained interaction between two individuals known to each other and on sufficiently good terms for one of them to have chosen the other as a partner. The two participants shared the roles of Addressor and Addressee. The average number of turns in the 2003 sessions was just under 300, so there were plenty of opportunities for both roles. The average number of words per turn ranged from 13 to 21. All the recordings show equally high participation by both speakers.

Ends

With respect to Ends, Hymes distinguishes between the goals of the individual participants and the overall purpose of the interaction. The adolescents had not chosen the Ends of the interaction but they were aware of the overall purpose of the study. The adolescents often showed concern about the success of the recording. To the extent that they collaborated in this enterprise they shared the goal of communicating with each other, and they had a mutual interest in the successful outcome. As part of the project the adolescents were to be video-taped in a simulation of a TV quiz competition in a professional

---

of the success of the project was the result of her good rapport with the adolescents. There are many joking references to her in the sessions, although the adolescents knew that she would hear these remarks. All the names in the transcripts have been replaced with pseudonyms.

recording studio. It is clear that this prospect provided a motivation for some (and probably all) of the adolescents.

There were also occasional references to the added benefit of missing classes. The consistency in the factors Setting, Scene, Participants, and Ends, provides a solid structural foundation for the collection of comparable data from the adolescents. There are no differences of age, social class, or power that might have contributed to an addressee effect. The recordings are for roughly the same length of time, so all the participants had an equal opportunity to speak. The remaining factors in Hymes' schema depend more upon the choices of the individual speakers. These are Message Form, Key, Norms of Interaction, and Genre.

Message form

> Only painstaking analysis of message form—how things are said—of a sort that indeed parallels and can learn from the intensity of literary criticism can disclose the depth and adequacy of the elliptical art that is talk.
>
> (Hymes, 1974: 55)

The bulk of communication in the adolescent sessions is carried on in what Chomsky (1957), in the days when he was still paying attention to E-language, called kernel sentences. The majority are simple, short statements, usually with a pronoun subject. The next most frequent syntactic type is questions. The message form is consequently simple and direct, with its focus on the addressor (the overall frequency of forms of *I* in the 2003 corpus is 58 per 1,000 words) and the addressee (the frequency of *you* is 32 per 1,000 words). There is little elaboration in the form of complex noun phrases and subordinate clauses are somewhat infrequent. The message form is thus simple, direct, and generally lacking in elaborated constructions.

Key

> Key is introduced to provide for the tone, manner, or spirit in which an act is done.
>
> (Hymes, 1974: 57)

One of the most impressive aspects of the recordings is the tone in which the speakers express themselves. This is very different from most speech samples obtained from adolescents under interview conditions or most situations where an adult was present. Three kinds of speech act show this: (1) use of taboo language; (2) threats; (3) reference to bodily functions.

Taboo language

The frequency with which some of the adolescents used taboo expressions suggests that they did not feel inhibited by the recording situation. There are 261 examples of the word *fuck* (in all its forms), 76 of *shit(e)*, 40 of *cunt* (usually with reference to a male), 23 of *bastard*, and 38 of *arse*. Two-thirds of the examples of taboo language occur in the boys' conversations but that means that the remaining third occur in the girls' conversations. For both boys and girls the favorite taboo word is *fuck*. Curiously, there is only one example of *bugger,* in one of the boys' conversations.

There are many references to swearing in the conversations, some of them teasing, others mock apologetic. There are some indications that certain examples of swearing are there to tease or shock the investigator, but many other examples have the ring of more normal usage, particularly when abusing the addressee.

Threats and insults

The participants often take the opportunity to abuse each other and to threaten bodily harm. Again, it is not only the boys who utter threats.

Bodily functions

Many of the references are to feeling hungry. More often they are expressions of urgent need to use the toilet. There are frequent references to farting and sometimes there is extended discussion of the subject. Ten out of the eighteen sessions in the 2003 recordings contain references to farting. In one session two boys engage in a spitting competition.

Instrumentalities

Under forms of speech Hymes refers to dialect as one of the factors. The Glasgow adolescents speak a form of urban Scots that is clearly marked phonologically (Stuart-Smith, 2003). This is obvious in the transcripts where the spelling of the words gives an indication of the local pronunciation: *ma* 'my,' *naw* 'no,' *nae* 'no,' *tae* 'to,' *dae* 'do,' *fitbaw* 'football' (i.e. soccer), *oot* 'out,' and *troosers* 'trousers.' There are also the morphological forms *–nae* for 'n't' in *doesnae, wasnae,* etc., and the lexical items *fae* 'from,' and *oer* 'over.' There would be no difficulty in identifying the form of speech from either the transcripts or the tapes themselves. These are recognizably working-class Glasgow adolescents. They are, of course, aware of their dialect. One speaker categorizes the other as "somebody who said 'ah' " for the first person pronoun *I*, a common working-class form in Glasgow. They are also aware that sometimes they use words that would not be familiar to those outside of the community, e.g. *ned* as a derogatory term for an individual.

Norms of interaction

As pointed out above, the adolescents feel free to criticize and even abuse each other in this kind of situation. But the interaction is not always competitive or aggressive. There are also places where the speakers are willing to exchange confidences in a more cooperative mood. The girls are capable of telling about very intimate matters as when two of them discuss having sex with a boy. There is also an expectation, at least among the girls, that secrets will be revealed.

When one girl tells her partner the name of the culprit, she whispers and the act of whispering somehow adds credibility to the idea that this is actually something she does not really want to be known widely. With the boys such explorations of preferences for the other sex are more likely to form the basis of teasing.

The norms of interaction for these sessions thus allow the communication of personal details. Despite the complaints about not knowing what to talk about and how slowly the time is passing, many of the participants succeed in communicating about their lives. As Erickson (2004: 5) points out, there is always the possibility of surprise when a speaker tells the hearer something that had not been known previously.

Genre

In addition to conversational exchanges of the kinds illustrated above three types of genre can be found in the sessions: Gossip, Narrative, and Word Play.

Gossip

Eggins and Slade define gossip as 'exchanging negative opinions and pejorative evaluations about the behaviour of a person who is absent' (1997: 12).

There are fewer examples of this in the 2003 recordings than might have been expected. One pair of middle-class girls in the 1997 recordings spent much of the time gossiping and there were also quite a few examples of gossip by the 1997 working-class girls.

Narrative

There are about a hundred narratives, most of them referring to embarrassing or illegal events. Some of the narratives are skeletal, with a minimum of background information. There are a few that are much better constructed narrative with effective use of quoted dialogue and evaluative devices.

Word Play

There are several instances where the adolescents indulge in various forms of word play. The simplest are successions of rhyming words. Other examples show a desire to play with names. Some of the examples seem very childish but the fact that they occurred reinforces the indications that the adolescents are not inhibited by the recording situation. It is often difficult to know what the purpose of the exchanges is, though it seems to have some of the competitive characteristics of sounding or playing the dozens (Labov, 1972b). They are joking and engaging in verbal dueling of various kinds and it is clear that rhyme and rhythm are important in this kind of word play. There is also a resemblance to the kinds of exchanges found by Lein and Brenneis (1978) in younger children. This word play shows a kind of cooperative interaction but is very different from the concern for the interlocutor that the older speakers often manifest.

Summary

The above sections have shown the Glasgow adolescents actively communicating under controlled conditions.[2] The speech samples are consequently appropriate for comparative analysis. There is no risk that the form of language will be affected by different recording situations, or such normally unexamined factors as an interviewer's age, gender, social class, or personality.

---

[2] Some examples are provided in the Appendix.

Quantitative analysis

For each of the transcripts a profile can be constructed on the basis of the speech recorded during the session. This is done by creating a concordance that includes all the words and constructions used in that session. The profiles can then be combined according to membership in a social category and comparisons made.

Many linguistic features do not fit easily into the usual category of linguistic variable in which certain forms are taken to be variants of each other with (in principle) an equal likelihood of occurring. An alternative approach to the quantitative analysis of discourse features is based on the following hypotheses:

1. All speakers have the same opportunity to use certain discourse features in the recording sessions.
2. Variation in the frequency of use of any of these features reflects a different discourse style.
3. Differences in using a discourse feature that correlate with membership of a social category such as age, gender, or social class show that such variation is not simply idiosyncratic.

(Macaulay, 2005a: 13)

In the 2003 recordings all the adolescents were working-class so the two social variables are age and gender.

Age differences

As was discussed in Chapter 1, age differences have been employed as a social factor in many variationist studies but the classification into age groups has varied. In the 1997 Glasgow study two age groups were recorded, adolescents age 13–14 and adults 40+, and the analysis revealed 20 statistically significant differences (Macaulay, 2005a: 158). This was a clearly polarized sample in terms of age. The 2003 Glasgow recordings of adolescents only do not provide such a clear contrast but the three age groups represent different stages in adolescence.

The youngest group in 2003 were still at primary school when they were recorded and thus not part of the same school community as the other two age groups, but the schools were in the same district and the 10–11-year-olds went on to the same secondary school as the others the following year. The 12–13-year-olds were in their first year at secondary school, while some of the 14–15-year-olds would leave school the following year. It is, therefore, not surprising

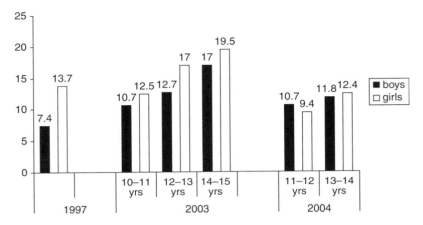

Figure 7.1: Total words used by working-class Glasgow adolescents by year and gender (in 1,000s)

that the three age groups display some speech differences, although the differences are not as marked as the contrast with adults in the 1997 recordings.

This results in a total corpus of just over 150,000 words. The analysis that follows will concentrate on the 2003 recordings. Since the adolescents are all working-class, the social factors for comparison are age and gender. The figures for each year are given in Figure 7 1.

It can be seen in Figure 7.1 that the older adolescents produce more speech than the younger ones though the differences are not statistically significant. (The statistical measure used on all frequency tests is the Mann-Whitney nonparametric test.) There is greater variation among the younger participants than in the other two age–groups. The recording of one pair of 10–11-year-old girls resulted in twice as much speech as either of the other pairs. Similarly, one pair of 10–11-year-old boys produced almost twice as much speech as one of the other pairs. There are no such extreme differences in the amounts recorded by the other age groups.

Questions occur with a frequency of 28 per 1,000 words in the 2003 recordings. This compares with a frequency of 19 questions per 1,000 words in the 1997 working-class sessions. In the 2003 recordings, the frequency of questions increases from 20 per 1,000 words for the youngest group to about 30 for the two older groups. Consistent with the 1997 recordings, the boys ask more questions (32 per 1,000 words) than the girls (24 per 1,000 words). Contrary to some views that boys are more competitive than girls, the frequency (and type) of questions shows the boys interacting in an equally cooperative fashion.

The questions are basically of three kinds: (a) personal (asking for information about the addressee); (b) impersonal (asking about someone or something not directly connected to the addressee; and (c) asking for clarification or confirmation (checking up that communication has been successful). Figure 7.2 (based on a sample of transcripts) shows age and gender differences in the kinds of questions asked.

Figure 7. 2 shows that girls ask more personal questions and are more likely to ask for confirmation or clarification while the boys are more like to ask questions that are impersonal. More striking, however, are the age differences, which can be seen in Figure 7.3.

Figure 7.3 shows that the youngest speakers ask the most questions about each other but also do the least checking up on whether communication has been achieved.

Of the content words in the 2003 corpus, the most frequent are nouns, which make up 14 percent of the total corpus, followed by verbs at 13 percent. Adjectives make up only 4 percent of the total and adverbs 3 percent.

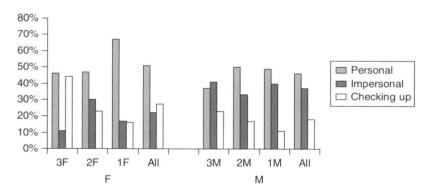

Figure 7.2: Percentage of questions by age and gender

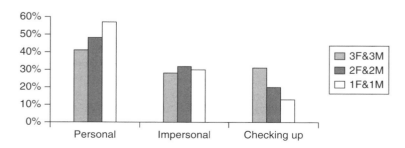

Figure 7.3: Percentage of questions by age group

(This is similar to the distribution in the 1997 recordings where nouns make up 11 percent, verbs 13 percent, adjectives 3 percent, and adverbs 2 percent.) Short words predominate with about 80 percent consisting of four letters or fewer. Only 7 percent of the words have seven or more letters. (Again, these figures are consistent with the 1997 recordings.)

Some of the important differences, however, are not quantitative but qualitative and the differences are greater among the boys than is the case with the girls. With the exception of a pair of 11-year-old girls who talk about which boys they like and why, the younger speakers do not talk much about their lives or what is happening around them. They talk about TV shows and films and engage in various forms of word play, including insulting each other. The 12–13-year-old boys are not very different from the younger boys and have almost no narratives in their exchanges. The 12–13-year-old girls, on the other hand, talk much more about their peers and situations in which they have interacted, and they have the highest proportion of narratives of any of the groups. The 14–15-year-olds, including the boys, are much more involved in talking about their lives than most of the younger adolescents and produce the most sustained narratives. (In an ethnographic study of 10–12-year-olds (Maybin, 2006) the best narratives are told by an 11-year-old girl and a 12-year-old boy, suggesting a similar age and gender difference.) The quantitative and qualitative differences presumably reflect the process of maturation, with the girls generally leading. Other age differences are linked to gender differences and will be dealt with below.

Gender differences

In each age group the girls speak more than the boys, but again the differences in the total number of words are not statistically significant. There are differences, however, in complexity. Although overall subordinate clauses are not very frequent, there are significant age and gender differences. The youngest age group have the fewest subordinate clauses, followed by the middle group, but almost half the subordinate clauses in the whole corpus are in the sessions with the oldest age group. In other words, the older adolescents use more complex syntax than the younger speakers. There are also gender differences. In the case of the two younger age groups, the girls use subordinate clauses approximately twice as often as the boys. In the oldest age group, however, the difference is greatly reduced, although it is still the case that the girls use subordination more frequently than the boys.

There are also gender differences in the use of proper nouns. In their conversations the adolescents make frequent references to their named peers. Both boys and girls name boys (15.2 per thousand words and 13.3 per thousand words, respectively) more often than they refer to girls by name. The girls, perhaps not surprisingly, name other girls (9.2 per thousand words) more frequently than the boys mention girls by name (3.1 per thousand words). Consistent with an earlier gender difference (Macaulay, 2005a), the boys are twice as likely as the girls to name physical locations (2.6 per thousand words vs. 1.2 per thousand words).

There is a significant difference in the proportion of the sessions devoted to sustained narratives. In the girls' sessions, approximately 38 percent of the transcripts consists of narratives. In the boys' sessions, taken as a whole, only about 8 percent of the transcripts consists of narrative. The difference, however, as pointed out above, comes from the two younger groups. The transcripts of the 14–15-year-old boys actually contain a slightly higher proportion of sustained narrative (23 percent) than do those of the 14–15-year-old girls (22 percent). The gender difference in the amount of narrative occurs only among the two younger groups.

The five most frequent lexical items used by the adolescents are *I, you, it, that* and *the*, which make up slightly over 10 percent of the total corpus. The use of the first two items varies widely in different sessions. The range of frequency for *I* is from 26.3 to 59.2 per 1,000 words (Mean 42.25; SD= 9.997) and for *you* from 13.6 to 53.8 per 1,000 words (Mean 27.56; SD= 10.853). The other three items, however, show much more consistent use throughout the sessions. The frequency of *it* ranges from 17.0 to 35.3 per 1,000 words (Mean 26.83; SD= 5.638), of *that* from 13.7 to 31.8 per 1,000 words (Mean 24.83; SD= 4.689), and of *the* from 13.8 to 34.9 per 1,000 words (Mean 21.46; SD= 5.365). The low standard deviation figures for these three items contrast with the much higher figures for the first two. These latter items are neutral with respect to topic.

In total, pronouns account for almost a fifth of the 2003 corpus (170 per 1,000 words). This is higher than the frequency of pronouns in the *Longman Grammar of Spoken English* (Biber, Johansson, Leech, Conrad and Finegan, 1999) where the frequency is only 144 per 1,000 words (calculated from table 4.33). The rank order of frequency for individual pronouns is almost identical in both corpora except that the Glasgow adolescents have fewer tokens of the third person plural pronoun *they*, which is the fourth most frequent pronoun in the Longman corpus but only sixth in the Glasgow corpus. An overwhelming majority of the pronouns occur in the subject form.

There are no significant gender differences in the use of the pronouns *you, he,* and *it* in the 2003 recordings but the girls use *she* (17 per 1,000 words) significantly more often than the boys (12 per 1,000 words). Even more significant is the difference in the use of the first person singular pronoun *I* with the girls using it more than twice as frequently (71 per 1,000 words) as the boys (33 per 1,000 words). This is a highly significant difference (p. < .001), similar to that found in the 1997 recordings. There is no gender difference in the use of the first person plural pronoun *we*, both groups using it with a frequency of 8 per 1,000 words. This is also consistent with the results from the 1997 recordings (Macaulay. 2005a: 132–3). Since the two sets of recordings were made under the same circumstances, the similarity gives added confidence in the earlier results.

The low frequency of adverbs is consistent with one of the more striking findings of earlier quantitative investigations (Macaulay, 1991a, 1995, 2002, 2005a). Those studies showed that there were social class and age differences in the use of certain types of adverbs. In 1997 the working-class adolescents used derived adverbs in -*ly* with a frequency of only 2.8 per 1,000 words. In 2003 the working-class adolescents used derived adverbs in -*ly* with an even lower frequency, 1.95 per 1,000 words. A simple comparison with the London COLT corpus (Stenström et al., 2002) will illustrate the situation. In the COLT corpus there are 1537 instances of the adverb *really*, a frequency of 3.6 per thousand words. In the 2003 Glasgow recordings there are 47 instances of *really*, a frequency of 0.53 per thousand words.

One of the Glasgow adolescents even uses a derived adverb pejoratively to illustrate the speech of a teacher:

Excerpt 7.1 (2003 2F)[3]
R: I hate her
      she's pure—
      right we try and dae like our work
      and she just pure rabbits on
      she talks through it
      she keeps saying 'Basically, basically'
      fucking what?
      does my heid in
L: no
      Miss Right
      she's a moany old cow

There are also similarities in the use of intensifiers between the two Glasgow sets of adolescents. In 1997, the working-class adolescents used *very* with a frequency of 0.14 per 1,000 words. In 2003, in the much larger corpus, there are only 17 examples of *very*, a frequency of 0.19 per 1,000 words. The similarity of these results is again remarkable, especially given the unconstrained nature of the conversations. (The figures for *quite* are 0.09

---

[3]The parenthetical references indicate the age and gender of the speakers in the 2003 recordings. The numbers refer to the three age groups and the letters to gender, e.g. (1M) = 10–11-year-old boys, (2F) = 12–13-year-old girls.

per 1,000 words in 1997 and 0.31 in 2003.) Replication of earlier findings is confirming evidence of the validity of the results (Campbell, 1969; Munroe and Munroe, 1991; Macaulay, 2003).

In 1997, instead of *very* the working-class adolescents used two nontraditional intensifiers *dead* and *pure*, as in the examples in Excerpt 7.2.

Excerpt 7.2 (1997)
a. I'd look **dead** funny without a fringe wouldn't I?
b. this is **dead** embarrassing
c. this is **pure** embarrassing
d. I was standing **pure** close to him

It is clear from the 2003 recordings that *dead* has ceased to be a popular intensifier for Glasgow working-class adolescents, occurring with a frequency of only 0.3 per 1,000 words compared with 2.2 in 1997. However, *pure* has increased in both frequency and in the range of contexts it can occur in (Macaulay, 2006b). In 1997 the working-class adolescents used *pure* with a frequency of 5.0 per 1,000 words; in the 2003 the frequency had more than doubled to 11.0 per thousand words.

With regard to non-traditional intensifiers, Figure 7.4 shows the dramatic falling off in the use of *dead* while *pure* remains very strong, though *so* is becoming more frequent.

Figure 7.5 gives the frequency of use of *pure* by year and gender. It can be seen that *pure* is used much more frequently by girls than by boys and this is statistically significant at the .05 level in 1997 and at the .01 level in 2003. The gender difference just fails to meet significance in 2004 but this is the result of the extremely high use (22.7 per 1,000 words) of *pure* by one 14-year-old boy. This is the highest frequency of any individual in the whole set. Without this outlier the gender difference would again be significant at .05 level. Figure 7.5 also shows a substantial increase in the use of *pure* from 1997 to 2003 and then a falling off in 2004. Although there are noticeable differences in the frequency for the three age groups in 2003, the use of *pure* by the 10–11-year-olds correlates with that of the 12–13-year-olds at the .05 level (Pearson = .635) and the use by the latter group correlates with that of the 14–15-year-olds at the .01 level (Pearson = .886).

In 2003 there is a new intensifier *heavy* that is used much less frequently than *pure* but may be replacing it in certain contexts, as shown in Excerpt 7.3.

Excerpt 7.3 (2003)
a. he's no pure **heavy** sexy (1F)
b. we think you're **heavy** cool man (2F)
c. Alan and Mary are **heavy** loved up (3F)
d. I'm going to **heavy** kill him anyway (3M)

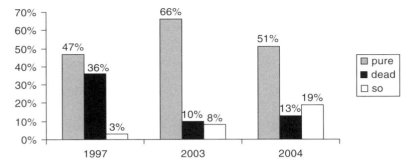

Figure 7.4: Main boosters used by Glasgow adolescents by year

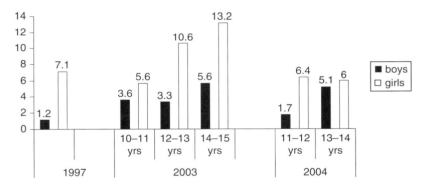

Figure 7.5: Use of *pure* by year and gender (per 1,000 words)

There is also a new term of approbation, *healthy*, that was apparently just beginning in 1997 but is used more widely in 2003.

Excerpt 7.4 (2003)
a. this is **healthy** man—sit and talk about shit (1M)
b. he's pure **healthy** but he's a wee fandang (2F)
c. I used to go "Phew he's **healthy**." (3F)
d. that's a **healthy** phone innit? (3M)

In examples 7.4b and 7.4c the meaning of *healthy* is 'good looking' (*fandang* is an annoying person).

Another epithet that is used more frequently in the 2003 recordings is *mad*. It can be used both positively and negatively.

Excerpt 7.5 (2003)
a. he got caught on a **mad** website (2F)

b.   I had a **mad** throat infection (2F)
c.   Gary bought a **mad** fitbaw man (2M)
d.   they're doing all **mad** tests (3M)

Figure 7.6 shows that *healthy* and *mad* are used more frequently by boys and that *heavy* and *healthy* are used more frequently by the older adolescents but there is no consistent age effect with *mad*. Figure 7.7 shows the age differences.

The use of *pure*, *heavy*, *healthy*, and *mad* shows that the Glasgow working-class adolescents have developed their own characteristic form of intensification.

The Glasgow adolescents also participate in the use of nontraditional quotatives (Blyth, Recktenwald and Wang, 1990; Romaine and Lange, 1991; Ferrara and Bell, 1995; Dougherty and Strassel, 1998; Igoe, Lamb, Gilman, Kim, 1999; Sanchez, and Charity, 1999; Tagliamonte and Hudson, 1999; Dailey-O'Cain, 2000; Macaulay, 2001a; Singler, 2001; Cukor-Avila, 2002; Tagliamonte and D'Arcy, 2004a, 2004b.; Buchstaller, 2006; Tagliamonte, 2007), and they have developed their own forms. The changes in the use of quotatives is shown in Table 7.1.

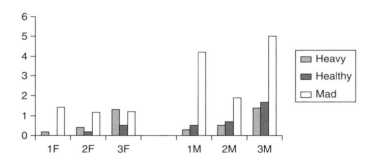

Figure 7.6: 2003 new intensifiers by year and gender (frequency by 1,000s)

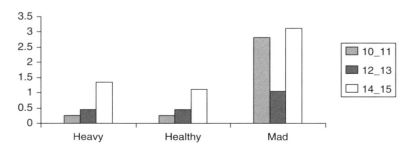

Figure 7.7: 2003 new intensifiers by year (frequency by 1,000s)

Table 7.1:   Distribution of quotative verbs used by Glasgow adolescents

	1997		2003	
	%	N	%	N
say	37	(46)	18	(131)
go	29	(37)	32	(232)
be like	5	(7)	9	(62)
be like that	10	(13)	25	(180)
go like that	9	(11)	5	(38)
be	1	(1)	0	(0)
think	2	(2)	1	(2)
done (that)	1	(1)	6	(43)
zero	5	(7)	4	(29)
other	3	(4)	1	(8)
Total		(129)		(725)

The most frequent quotative in 2003 is *go*, contrary to the situation in Canada reported by Tagliamonte and D'Arcy (2004a, 2004b) where *go* has practically ceased to be used. The percentage use of *go* in Glasgow has increased from 29 percent to 32 percent, but there are age differences. In the youngest group (10–11) only 8 percent of the quotatives are *go* compared with 43 percent in the oldest group (14–15) and 49 percent in the middle group (12–13). However, the greatest increase is in the frequency of *be like that*. This form was first reported in Macaulay (2001a) as used by working-class girls and one working-class woman. Examples from the 2003 recordings are given in Excerpt 7.6.

Excerpt 7.6
a.   I was like that "Shut up"(2F)
b.   Goldie was like that "What you talking about?" (3M)
c.   I'm like that "Oh it's lovely" (3F)
d.   my ma was like that "You bastard" (3M)

Table 7.2 shows the frequencies with which each age group in 2003 used the various quotatives.

The figures in Table 7.2 show that *go like that* is not used by the oldest group (there is only one example from one 15-year-old girl and none from the 14–15-year-old boys). In contrast, among the 14–15 year-olds the use of *be like that* has increased for both boys and girls. More significantly, the oldest age group is responsible for 91 percent of the examples of *be like*. In

Table 7.2 Quotatives used most frequently by Glasgow adolescents in 2003 (freq. = per 1,000 words)

	be like that	be like	go like that	say	go	done (that)
10-11-yr-old girls	0.24	0	**1.68**	0.4	1.60	0
10-11-yr-old boys	0.37	0.09	0.93	1.3	0.56	0
12-13-yr-old girls	4.40	0.29	0.35	2.76	**5.94**	0.47
12-13-yr-old boys	0.79	0.79	0	**1.47**	1.10	0
14-15-yr-old girls	**3.72**	2.35	0.05	1.53	3.27	0
14-15-yr-old boys	1.64	0.62	0	1.23	1.85	**2.33**

1997 the working-class girls used *be like* with a frequency of 0.8 per 1,000 words and the working-class boys did not use it at all, so the increase in use by the 14–15-year-old girls to 2.14 per 1,000 words and by the boys to 0.62 per 1,000 words shows a marked change. In each age group the girls are twice as likely to use *go* as the boys. As Levey (2008) found was the case with London preadolescents, the boys are much more likely to use *go* with non-lexicalized sounds (36 percent of the instances of *go/went*) than the girls (7 percent).

In 1997 there were four examples of *done that* as a quotative (Macaulay, 2001a: 9). In 2003 there were 43 examples of *done* as a quotative, as illustrated in Excerpt 7.7.

Excerpt 7.7
a. and he done that "Awf man we're all game" (3M)
b. and he done that "I'm no fae this area" (3M)
c. he done that "Have you been a Blues fan?" (3M)
d. and we done that to him "What you doing?" (3M)

There are 13 examples of *done that*, all from 14–15-year-old boys and one from a 14–15-year-old girl, but there are also 29 examples of *done* alone, as in Excerpt 7.8.

Excerpt 7.8
a. my auntie done "Gie us it" (2F)
b. and I done "Want to go and tell somebody?" (2F)
c. and Bob's done "Aye what you gonnae do?" (3M)
d. he done "It's like a dream come true" (3M)

Most of the examples come from 14–15-year-old boys but there are 8 examples from 12–13-year-old girls. The fact that 60 percent of the *done* forms (including all those produced by the 12–13-year-old girls) occur without *that* suggests that the need for the deictic pronoun is lessening. If this is correct, then it is reasonable to suppose that the forms *go like that* and *be like that* may soon become obsolescent. As the 10–11-year-olds grow older they will probably adapt to the prevailing standards of their elders. Thus, the predominance of *go like that* in the youngest group need not be taken as an indication of a change in progress.

The evidence from the use of quotatives suggests that there has been some outside influence on the Glasgow adolescents though they continue to create an individual pattern that is distinct from those found elsewhere. This, as outlined above, is most obvious in their use of the intensifiers *pure, heavy, healthy,* and *mad* (Macaulay, 2006b, 2008). There is, however, no sign that they are adopting the forms *cool* or *totally*. The latter is hardly surprising given the limited use of derived adverbs in *–ly*. Both boys and girls, however, frequently *man* as a punctor as in Excerpt 7.9.

Excerpt 7.9
a.   LM's a pure pain in the arse man (3M)
b.   ah hate this school man (3F)

In 1997 the frequency was 3.5 per thousand words, in 2003 the frequency has more than tripled to 11.6 per thousand words. Figure 7.8 shows that at each age boys use *man* more often than girls, but also that for both boys and girls the frequency increases with age.

There are two other expressions have apparently slipped in from outside. The first is *oh my God* which does not occur in the working-class conversations in 1997, though there are two examples in the conversations of the middle-class girls. In the 2003 working-class girls' conversations there are 28 examples of *oh my God*, two-thirds of them in the 12–13-year-old group and the remainder in the 14–15-year-old group. There are no examples in the conversations of the 10–11-year-old girls. There are only two examples in the boys' conversations, one each in the 10–11 and 12–13-year-old groups.

The frequency with which the expression *oh my God* occurs in the conversations of the older girls in the 2003 conversations is quite striking. The absence of this expression from the 1997 adolescent and adult working-class conversations indicates a change that is unlikely to have happened without some influence from Valleyspeak.

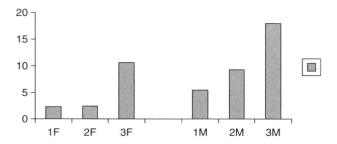

Figure 7.8: 2003 frequency of *man* as a punctor (per 1,000 words)

Another expression that has greatly increased in frequency is *or something*. Terminal tags (Dines, 1980) are common in many forms of Scottish working-class speech (Macaulay, 1985, 1991a) but *or something* is not common, though occasionally a speaker will use *or something like that*. In the 1997 recordings there are only 17 examples of *or something*, a frequency of 0.81 per thousand words. In the 2003 recordings there are 187 examples of *or something*, a frequency of 1.88 per thousand words in the boys' conversations and of 2.23 in the girls' conversations. Again, it seems unlikely that this will have happened without some influence from Valleyspeak. There are a few examples suggesting that the youngest girls are aware of the use of *whatever* as a discourse marker, but no sign of it in the sessions with the older adolescents.

Both girls and boys seem to be innovators. The girls lead in their use of *be like* while the boys are the leaders in the use of *done (that)*. Girls are the leaders in the use of *pure* but the boys use *mad* and *healthy* more frequently than the girls (Macaulay, 2008). Only the girls have adopted *oh my God* but both boys and girls are using *or something*.

It is a mystery how forms such as *be like* have spread from an assumed Californian origin to the rest of the United States and elsewhere. The media would appear to be an obvious vehicle but that does not explain why some features are adopted and others ignored. In the 2003 conversations there are no clues as to possible influences from the media. Such references as there are concern British television programs that do not provide a model for the adoption of transatlantic forms. The evidence from the Glasgow conversations suggests that adolescents do not succumb easily to the influence of outside models but choose those features that for some reason attract them, adapting them in novel ways, while they ignore other features that are current elsewhere.

Conclusion

The above account of the 2003 recordings shows that it is possible to identify age and gender differences in the use of discourse features on the basis of relatively short samples of speech recorded under controlled circumstances. There are no differences in the setting, scene, participant role, motivation, or message form that might distort the results. The recordings give a rare example of adolescents interacting with each other without the physical presence of an adult (though the tape-recorder serves as a surrogate overhearer). The liveliness of the exchanges and the apparent frankness with which the participants address each other (including abusive remarks) suggest that these recordings are suitable material for the investigation of sociolinguistic variation. Recordings of this type are particularly important for the study of discourse features that are less likely to emerge in interviews, least of all in interviews of adolescents by adults. The recordings also provide 'good data' on phonological and morphological features that are being analyzed elsewhere. While it will not always be able to control the conditions as narrowly, the success of this project and that of the earlier 1997 study (Macaulay, 2005a) demonstrate the value of the technique.

Questions for discussion

What are the advantages and disadvantages of collecting data by the method illustrated in this chapter?

What other discourse features do you think could be profitably examined?

Afterword

The preceding pages have examined only a fraction of the work that has been produced in sociolinguistics in the past fifty years, but it is enough to show the wide range of techniques and methods that have been employed in the variationist framework employing quantitative methods. There is every reason to be optimistic that future investigators will build on this framework and reveal more of the systematic nature of language variation. It will be helpful for purposes of evaluation and comparison, however, if these investigators are as explicit as possible about their methods. Ruth Wodak has emphatically stated the standard to be met:

> Methodology, in my view, should be retroductive; that is, any research procedure and device should be transparent and explicit, and thus allow recipients to trace and understand the operationalization and interpretation of results.
>
> (Wodak 2006: 609)

There is a useful example of explicitness in the contrast between two replications of Labov's (1963) study of centralization on Martha's Vineyard. Blake and Josey (2003) report on an investigation based on interviews carried out by Josey on Martha's Vineyard in 2003. They claim, on the basis of acoustic analysis of token of the (ay) diphthong, that centralization has lost the social significance that Labov had found in 1962. Pope, Meyerhoff and Ladd (2007) report on a second investigation on Martha's Vineyard based on interviews carried out by Pope in 2001–2. Pope et al. found that centralization is still socially significant on the island and similar to what Labov had found forty years earlier.

Pope et al. point out the methodological differences between the two investigations that might account for the discrepancy. In particular, they point out differences between the two investigators and the manner in which they collected their samples:

> Josey's study was essentially restricted to speakers from one Community, Chilmark, whereas our study, to the greatest extent

possible, involved an exact replication of Labov's sample, interviewing
speakers throughout the island.

(Pope et al. 2007: 625)

They go on to point out that Josey identified her speakers on the basis of
network contacts in the Chilmark region through the family for which she
was employed as an au pair. In contrast, Pope stayed in the island's youth
hostel and hitchhiked to travel from one town to the other, during two short
visits, one in the summer and one in winter. Pope et al. comment:

It seems likely that working and living, during the early part of the tour-
ist season, with a family who can afford an au pair may have provided
Josey with different contacts from those that [Pope] made when hitch-
hiking around the island, sometimes in the middle of winter.

(Pope et al. 2007: 625)

Pope et al. go on to make a more speculative observation:

it is possible that the two fieldworkers represented rather different
figures to the people they interviewed, and as a consequence may have
elicited different norms. Josey's contacts with a well-to-do family may
have given her a rather different perceived social role from [Pope's]
status as a student hitchhiker from abroad. A related factor is that
Josey's General American accent may have triggered accommodation
toward noncentralized variants, whereas [Pope's] British accent would
have been less likely to have this effect.

(Pope et al. 2007: 625)

It is rare in research reports to find discussion of factors such as those
Pope et al. examine, but it is obvious that they can affect the quality of the
speech recorded. It is also an example of a methodology that is "transparent and explicit" in the sense of the quotation from Wodak (2006) cited
above.

More transparency of this kind will help establish variationist sociolinguistics on a firm basis.

No doubt future investigators will develop new methods but a strong
foundation has been laid for further work that will provide more information
on the nature of language variation. It is to be hoped that, as sociolinguistics expands as a field, there will be many more projects building on this
foundation.

The aim of the present work has been to examine the methodology employed in variationist sociolinguistic projects in the hope that this will be helpful in two ways. The first is to encourage those citing the results of earlier studies to make a careful examination of the basis on which any claims are made before accepting the conclusions of the investigators. The paradigm case is the enormous impact the work of Basil Bernstein had on educational policy despite the inadequacy of the empirical basis for his claims (see Macaulay 2005a for an examination of Bernstein's evidence).

A second plea is that future investigators will be as explicit as possible about their methods, including listing the data on which the calculations have been based, as in Macaulay (1977, 1991, 2005a) and Milroy (1980). If space does not permit the inclusion of such material in the printed version, the figures could be posted on a website.

Given the resources and effort that collecting samples of speech involves, it is unfortunate that so much of this material remains unanalyzed. I hope that some investigators will follow Jane Stuart-Smith's generous example in making her materials available to me in a form that allowed me to investigate the questions that interested me (Macaulay 2005a; Chapter 7 above).

Appendix

The following are excerpts from the transcripts illustrating some of the ways in which the speakers interact.

Comments on the recording situation

Excerpt A.1 (2003 3M)[1]
L: how are we supposed to talk?
R: don't know
    pure fucking dolly man
L: aye but how could they sit
    how can other people sit
    and have a long conversation?
R: don't know man
    they're geeks

Excerpt A.2 (2003 1M)
L: Stewart sit doon
    I cannae wait man til we go to the mad studio thing
R: I want school to finish
L: it's gonnae be shit-hot
R: what's the studio thing?
    what thing?
L: we're going to the— we're no gonnae be on telly
    but with aw the crew cunts and aw
    that are aw going to be there and we just
R: with us
L: aye and a mad challenge thing gonnae be shithot

Excerpt A.3 (2003 2F)
L: I'm pure heavy bored

---

[1] The parenthetical references indicate the age and gender of the speakers in the 2003 recordings. The numbers refer to the three age groups and the letters to gender, e.g. (1M) = 10–11-year-old boys, (2F) = 12–13-year-old girls.

R: I know
    better than being in Science but innit?
L: yeah
R: just sitting talking a load of crap
L: relaxing (*both laugh*)

Examples of taboo language

Excerpt A.4 (2003 1M)
L: mad Stewart
    you fucking picking your nose
R: what was I daeing?
    was I picking my—
L: you big fucking speccy bastard you picked your nose
R: that's big talk coming fae somebody who said 'ah' [for /] and
    aw that
L: mad Stewart your balls are still plastered to your arse
R: ah and your arse is coming off
L: oh man
R: it wasnae that funny
L: aye it fucking was
R: aw how is that?
    how's it funny?

Excerpt A.5 (2003 3F)
R: em who the fuck are we gonnae go oot with tonight then?
L: exactly
R: who can we get tae come oot with us?
L: nae cunt

Examples of threats

Excerpt A.6 (2003 2M)
L: (*inaudible*) punch utter shite out of you
    honest I will
R: I'll punch you
L: no I will batter you though but
    no
    seriously
R: I'll batter you.

Excerpt A.7 (2003 2F)
L: listen I'm gonna piss on your face

I'm gonna fart in your mouth
and I'm gonna shit all over these walls bitch

Excerpt A.8 (2003 2F)
L: sit and talk you bitch
    fore I batter you

Example of personal comments

Excerpt A.9 (2003 2F)
L: Josie you are heavy smelling
R: (*laughs*)
L: I've never known a lassie tae fart as much as you
R: (*laughs*) (*inaudible*) fart
L: aye ye did
R: so I did
L: you did Josie
R: aye so I did
L: (*makes fart sound*) there you go again man
R: (*laughs*) that's you
L: man your ar— your bum has got a (*inaudible*) trumpet or
    something up it
R: (*makes fart sound*) Cheryl
L: (*makes fart sound*) oh roo— I want oot of here
    let me oot

Reference to local speech variety

Excerpt A.10 (2003 2M)
L: you've got my patter
R: pure neddy mouth
    (*laughs*)
    people that aren't from Glasgow aren't going to have a clue
    what we're talking about are they?
L: from Glasgow?
R: no
    people that aren't from Glasgow won't
    because it's only like people from Glasgow
    that use 'ned' as a word
L: townies
R: townies are from England you dick
    (*Ned* is a pejorative term for badly behaved individuals.)

Examples of girls talking about relationships

Excerpt A.11 (2003 1F)
R: do ye like going oot with David?
L: s'awright
    do you like being with Joe?
R: aye
L: I do like being with David actually
R: I really like going oot with Joe
    I don't know why
    I just dae
L: aye but you've liked Joe for—for—
    well I dunno for pure ages but
R: you says on Thursday you pure really liked David
L: aye I know but I mean
R: I know it's hard to say you don't but

Excerpt A.12 (2003 1F)
R: I was determined to go up and give him a cuddle or something
    so anyway I just couldnae
    I just could—
    no I couldnae
L: oh you should've
    you should've
    cause they were there
    ah I wouldnae let them put you off Maureen
R: no (*inaudible*)
    it wasnae because of them
    I dunno
    it was like he was standing like that on
    the way had his back to the wall
    so I couldn't exactly cuddle him eh

Example of gossip

Excerpt A.13 (2003 2F)
R: who— who was it then?
    who?
    how?
    tell me?
L: no cos you'll tell somebody
R: Cheryl I've told you hunners of secrets
    and you haven't even told me wan yet
L: I cannae tell you
    it's really embarrassing

R: I even tell you on the phone and everything
L: pure embarrassing
promise ye willnae tell anybody?
(When she tells the name, she whispers)

Example of teasing

Excerpt A.14 (2003 2M)
R: who dae you fancy Joe?
L: depends on maself
R: aye
L: uh
R: well who do you?
L: that wee (*inaudible*)
R: Joe Hudson fancies—Joe Hudson fancies Stephanie Wright
L: and you used tae
R: aye ah used tae mate
L: you still dae don't ye?
R: no
L: ah thought you did
R: aye well you thought wrong
L: you st— you dae but
R: no ah don't
L: ach

Example of nonsensical word play

Excerpt A.15 (2003 M1)
R: Miss Maguire pee'd in the fire
the fire stopped
she pee'd in the pot
the pot was too wide
she pee'd in the Clyde
and aw them fishes went up her backside
L: she opened up her legs
I saw her bum
it was fantastic
it was made of plastic
I saw your dad
he opened up his legs
I saw his fannypad
it was fantastic
it was made of plastic

I saw—I saw your son
he opened up his legs
I saw his bum
it was fantastic
it was made of plastic
R: oh yeah
L: I saw your sister
she opened up her legs
I saw her blister
it was fantastic
it was made of plastic
yeah yeah
I saw Mark
he opened up his legs
I saw a park
it was fantastic
it was made of plastic
yeah yeah

Examples of narrative

Excerpt A.16 (2003 1M)
L: guess what
see ma big brother?
R: aye
L: Right
he was in the room
right
he was in ma room with his bird
his bird
right
and his bird was on the bed
and so was he
and he was sitting poking her
and we walked intae the room man
we opened the door
and aw you seen was him flying up
and she pult her troosers up
it was funny
so it was man
it was heavy funny man

Excerpt A.17 (2003 2F)
L: I hate him

I've been in late three times or something
he was like that "I want to see your parents up"
I went hame and told my ma
my ma was like that "Right, I'll go up and see the old bastard
see what he's got to say to me
I'll tell him where to go"
R: *(laughs)*
L: I'm like that "You cannae tell the—the headmaster where to go
he'll kick me oot o school"
and she went "so?
we'll find you another school"
I went "I don't want to find another school"
she went "You will"
oh my God
I'm no leaving aw my pals

Excerpt A.18 (2003 3M)
R: playing badminton
when was it?
two weeks ago
Robson "dare you to hit her"
and I was like that "what?"
and he goes, "I dare you tae hit her
I'm "what you mean?"
and he goes "with the shuttle"
so came over man
and I went "WHACK!"
right in the middle of the foredome
I was only like see hitting it with wee dink shots
on to the net and like that man
and it's come over and I went "smash"
and it's hit her right in the dome
I was in stitches
L: you've nae chance with her now Steve
R: no she was laughing mate
she says "I like your cock"
I went "what?"
L: I like your what?
your shuttlecock?
R: she done "that was a bad shot"
I was like that "I dinnae mean it"
and she's like, "aye, I bet ye never"
L: she is actually all right in't she?
R: mhmm
just a bit posh

Excerpt A.19 (2003 3F)

L: Ah remember when Miss McCartney took ma phone aff me
    on Friday
    and ah called her a cow
R: did ye?
L: aye
    cause she went "Switch your phone off"
    and ah was—ah was waiting on ma Ma tae text back
    cause ah said "Mum will you be in after school
    ah've no got ma keys"
    and ah had tae wait
    and she'll text back
    Miss McGrath grabbed ma phone aff me
    and ah went "miss see that"
    ah says " ah need tae wait till ma Ma texts back"
    and she went "No"
    and done that in ma face
    and switched it aff
    and ah went "cow"
    and she went "AH HEARD THAT"
    and she was pure shouting at me
    and she went "get in ma office"
    and then ah just growled
    and she went "no
    get tae your class
    get in ma office at half three
    so you can get your phone back"
    but ah saw the phone in the school office
    and ah just told them tae give it back
    ah never went
R: (laughs)
L: was pure scared man

References

Aijmer, Karin and Bengt Altenberg. 1991. *English Corpus Linguistics: Studies in Honour of Jan Svartvik*. London: Longman.

Argyle, Michael. 1994. *The Psychology of Social Class*. London: Routledge.

Azoulay, Katya Gibel. 1997. *Black, Jewish, and Interracial: It's not the Color of your Skin but the Race of your Kin*. Durham: Duke University Press.

Bailey, Guy and Jan Tillery. 2004. "Some sources of divergent data in sociolinguistics." In Carmen Fought (ed.) *Sociolinguistic Variation: Critical Reflections*, 11–30. New York: Oxford University Press.

Bailey, Guy, Tom Wikle, Jan Tillery, and Lori Sand. 1991. "The apparent time construct." *Language Variation and Change* 3: 241–64.

Bakhtin, M.M. 1981. *The Dialogic Imagination: Four essays by M.M. Bakhtin*, (ed.) Michael Holquist, trans. Caryl Emerson and Michael Holquist. Austin: University of Texas Press.

Barth, Fredrik. 1969. *Ethnic Groups and Boundaries: The Social Organization of Culture Differences*. Boston: Little, Brown.

Bauman, Richard. 1983. *Let your Words be Few: Symbolism of Speaking and Silence among Seventeenth-century Quakers*. Cambridge: Cambridge University Press.

Bayley, Robert. 2002. The quantitative pattern. In J.K. Chambers, Peter Trudgill, and Natalie Schilling-Estes (eds.) *The Handbook of Language Variation and Change*, 117–41. Oxford: Blackwell.

Bell, Allan. 1984. "Language style as audience design." *Language in Society* 13. 145–204.

Bell, Allan. 2001. Back in style: Reworking audience design. In Penelope Eckert and John R. Rickford (eds.) *Style and Sociolinguistic Variation*, 139–69. Cambridge: Cambridge University Press.

Bell, Allan and Gary Johnson. 1997. Towards a sociolinguistics of style. *University of Pennsylvania Working Papers in Linguistics* 4: 1–21.

Berdan, Robert H. 1975. On the nature of linguistic variation. Unpublished PhD dissertation, University of Texas at Austin.

Berdan, Robert H. 1978. Multidimensional analysis of vowel variation. In David Sankoff (ed.) *Linguistic Variation: Models and Methods*, 149–60. New York: Academic Press.

Bernstein, Basil. 1962. Social class, linguistic codes, and grammatical elements. *Language and Speech* 5, 31–46.

Biber, Douglas and Edward Finegan. 1988. "Adverbial stance types in English." Discourse Processes 11: 1–34.

Biber, Douglas, Stig Johansson, Geoffrey Leech, Susan Conrad, and Edward Finegan. 1999. *Longman Grammar of Spoken and Written English.* Harlow: Longman.

Blake, Renee and Meredith Josey. 2003. The /ay/ diphthong in a Martha's Vineyard community: What can we say 40 years after Labov? *Language in society* 32: 451–85.

Blyth, Carl, Jr., Sigrid Recktenwald and Jenny Wang. 1990. "I'm like, 'Say what?!': A new quotative in American oral narrative." *American Speech* 65. 304–7.

Bortoni-Ricardo, S.M. 1985. *The Urbanization of Rural Dialect Speakers: A Sociolinguistic Study in Brazil.* Cambridge: Cambridge University Press.

Bourdieu, Pierre. 1991. *Language and Symbolic Power.* Cambridge: Polity Press.

Brown, Penelope and Colin Fraser. 1979. "Speech as a marker of situation." In Klaus R. Scherer and Howard Giles (eds.) *Social Markers in Speech,* 33–62. Cambridge: Cambridge University Press.

Bucholz, Mary 2000. "The politics of transcription." *Journal of Pragmatics* 32: 1439–65.

Buchstaller, Isabelle. 2006. "Social stereotypes, personality traits and regional perception displaced: Attitudes towards the 'new' quotatives in the U.K." *Journal of Sociolinguistics* 10: 362–81.

Cameron, Deborah. 1985. *Feminism and Linguistic Theory.* London: Macmillan.

Campbell, D.T. 1969. "Reforms as experiments". *American Psychologist* 25: 409–29.

Cannadine, David (1998) *Class in Britain.* London: Penguin.

Cedergren, Henrietta and David Sankoff. 1974. Variable rules: Performance as a statistical reflection of competence. *Language* 50: 233–55.

Chafe, Wallace. 1994. *Discourse, Consciousness, and Time: The Flow and Displacement of Conscious Experience in Speaking and Writing.* Chicago: University of Chicago Press

Chambers, J.K. 1988. "Acquisition of phonological variants." In Alan R. Thomas (ed.) *Methods in Dialectology,* 650–65. Clevedon, Avon: Multilingual Matters.

Chambers. J.K. 1994. An introduction to dialect topography. *English World-Wide* 15: 35–53.

Chambers, J.K. 1995. *Sociolinguistic Theory.* Oxford: Blackwell.

Cheshire, Jenny, 1982. *Variation in an English Dialect.* Cambridge: Cambridge University Press.

Cheshire, Jenny. 1999. "Taming the vernacular: Some repercussions for the study of syntactic variation and spoken grammar." *Cuadernos de Filología Inglesa* 8: 59–80.

Cheshire, Jenny. 2007. "Discourse variation, grammaticalisation and stuff like that." *Journal of Sociolinguistics* 11: 155–93.

Cheshire, Jenny, Paul Kerswill, and Ann Williams. 1999. *The Role of Adolescents in Dialect Levelling.* Ref. R000236180. Final report submitted to the Economic and Social Science Research Council.

Chomsky, Noam. 1957. *Syntactic Structures.* The Hague: Mouton.

Cichoki, Wladyslaw. 1988. "Uses of dual scaling in social dialectology: Multidimensional analysis of vowel variation." In Alan R. Thomas (ed.) *Methods in Dialectology,* 187–97. Clevedon, Avon: Multilingual Matters.

Coates, Jennifer. 1996. *Women Talk*. Oxford: Blackwell.

Coates, Jennifer. 2003. *Men Talk: Stories in the Making of Masculinities*. Oxford: Blackwell.

Coombs, Clyde Hamilton. 1964. *A Theory of Data*. New York: Wiley.

Cornips, Leonie. 1998. Syntactic variation, parameter, and social distribution. *Language Variation and Change* 10: 1–21.

Cornips, Leonie and Karen P. Corrigan (eds.) 2005. *Syntax and variation: Reconciling the Biological and the Social*. Amsterdam: John Benjamins.

Coupland, Justine. 2000. *Small Talk*. Harlow, Essex: Longman.

Coupland, Nikolas. 1980. "Style-shifting in a Cardiff work setting." *Language in Society*, 9: 1–12.

Coupland, Nikolas. 1988. *Dialect in Use: Sociolinguistic Variation in Cardiff English*. Cardiff: University of Wales Press.

Coupland, Nikolas. 2002. Language, situation, and the relational self: Theorizing dialect style. In J.K. Chambers, Peter Trudgill, and Natalie Schilling-Estes (eds.) *The Handbook of Language Variation and Change,* 185–210. Oxford: Blackwell.

Coupland, Nikolas. 2007. *Style: Language Variation and Identity*. Cambridge: Cambridge University Press.

Coupland, Nikolas, Justine Coupland, and Howard Giles. 1991. *Language Society and the Elderly: Discourse, Identity and Ageing*. Oxford: Blackwell.

Crompton, Rosemary, Fiona Devine, Mike Savage, and John Scott, (eds.) 2000. *Renewing Class Analysis*. Oxford: Blackwell/The Sociological Review.

Cukor-Avila, Patricia. 2002. "*She say, she go, she be like*: Verbs of quotation over time in African American Vernacular English." *American Speech* 77. 3–31.

Cukor-Avila, Patricia and Guy Bailey. 2001. The effects of the race of the interviewer on sociolinguistic fieldwork. *Journal of Sociolinguistics* 5: 254–70

Dailey-O'Cain, Jennifer. 1997. "Canadian raising in a midwestern U.S. city." *Language Variation and Change* 9.107–20.

Dailey-O'Cain, Jennifer. 2000. "The sociolinguistic distribution and attitudes toward focuser *like* and quotative *like*." *Journal of Sociolinguistics*

Dannenberg, Clare J. 2002. *Sociolinguistic Constructs of Ethnic Identity: The Syntactic Delineation of an American Indian English*. (Publication No. 87 of the American Dialect Society.) Durham: Duke University Press.

D'Arcy, Alexandra. 2007. "*Like* and language ideology: Disentangling fact from fiction". *American Speech* 82: 386–419.

Dines, Elizabeth R. 1980. Variation in discourse – "and stuff like that." *Language in Society* 9: 13–31.

Dittmar, Norbert. 1988. Foreword to the series "Sociolinguistics and language contact." In Norbert Dittmar and Peter Schlobinski (eds.) *The Sociolinguistics of Urban Vernaculars: Case studies and their Evaluation,* ix–xii. Berlin: de Gruyter.

Dittmar, Norbert. 1995. "Theories of sociolinguistic variation in the German context." In Patrick Stevenson (ed.) *The German Language and the Real World,* 135–60. Oxford: Oxford University Press.

Docherty, Gerard J., Paul Foulkes, James Milroy, Lesley Milroy, and David Walshaw. 1997. "Descriptive adequacy in phonology: A variationist perspective." *Journal of Linguistics* 33: 275–310.

Dorian, Nancy C. 1994. "Stylistic variation in a language restricted to private-sphere use. In Douglas Biber and Edward Finegan (eds.) *Sociolinguistic Perspectives on Register*, 217–32. New York: Oxford University Press.

Dougherty, Kevin A. and Stephanie M. Strassel. 1998. A new look at variation in and perception of American English quotatives. Paper given at NWAV-27, University of Georgia, October 1998.

Douglas-Cowie, Ellen. 1978. "Linguistic code-switching in a Northern Irish village: Social interaction and social ambition." In Peter Trudgill (ed.) *Sociolinguistic Patterns in British English*, 37–51. London: Edward Arnold.

Dressler, Richard A. and Roger J. Kreuz. 2000. "Transcribing oral discourse: A survey and a model system." *Discourse Processes* 29: 25–36.

Dubois, Betty Lou and Isabel Crouch. 1975. The question of tag questions in women's speech: They don't really use more of them, do they? *Language in Society* 4: 289–94.

DuBois, John W., Stephan Schuetze-Coburn, Susanna Cumming, and Danae Paolina. 1993. "Outline of discourse transcription." In Jane A. Edwards and Martin D. Lampert (eds.) *Talking Data: Transcription and Coding in Discourse Research*, 3–31. Hillsdale, NJ: Lawrence Erlbaum.

Dubois, Sylvie. 1993. Extension particles, etc. *Language Variation and Change 4*: 179–203.

Dubois, Sylvie and Barbara M. Horvath. 1998. "Let's tink about dat: Interdental fricatives in Cajun English." *Language Variation and Change* 10: 245–61.

Eckert, Penelope. 1989. *Jocks and Burnouts: Social Categories and Identity in the High School*. New York: Teachers College.

Eckert, Penelope. 1996. "Age as a sociolinguistic variable." In Florian Coulmas (ed.) *Handbook of Sociolinguistics*, 151–67. Oxford: Blackwell.

Eckert, Penelope. 2000. *Linguistic Variation as Social Practice*. Oxford: Blackwell.

Eckert, Penelope. 2003. "Social variation in America." In Dennis R. Preston (ed.) *Needed Research in American Dialects*. Publication of the American Dialect Society No. 88. 99–121.

Eckert, Penelope and John R. Rickford (eds.) 2001. *Style and Sociolinguistic Variation*. Cambridge: Cambridge University Press.

Eckert, Penelope and Sally McConnell-Ginet. 1992. "Think practically and look locally: Language and gender as community-based practice." *Annual Review of Anthropology* 21, 461–90.

Edwards, Walter F. 1992. Sociolinguistic behaviour in a Detroit inner city black neighbourhood. *Language in Society* 21: 93–115.

Eggins, Suzanne and Diana Slade. 1997. *Analyzing Casual Conversation*. London: Cassell.

Elliott, Nancy. 2000. A sociolinguistic study of rhoticity in American film speech from the 1930s to the 1970s. Unpublished PhD dissertation, Indiana University.

Erickson, Frederick. 2004. *Talk and Social Theory: Ecologies of Speaking and Listening in Everyday Life.* Cambridge: Polity press.

Fabb, Nigel. 2002. *Language and Literary Structure: The Linguistic Analysis of Form in Verse and Narrative.* Cambridge: Cambridge University Press.

Fasold, Ralph W. 1972. *Tense Marking in Black English.* Washington, DC: Center for Applied Linguistics.

Fasold, Ralph W. and Dennis R. Preston. 2007. "The psycholinguistic unity of inherent variability: Occam whips out his razor." In Robert Bayley and Ceil Lucas (eds.) *Sociolinguistic Variation: Theories, Methods, and Applications,* 45–69. Cambridge: Cambridge University Press.

Feagin, Crawford. 1979. *Variation and Change in Alabama English: A Sociolinguistic Study of the White Community.* Washington, DC: Georgetown University Press.

Ferrara, Kathleen and Barbara Bell. 1995. "Sociolinguistic variation and discourse function of constructed dialogue introducers: The case of be+like." *American Speech* 70. 265–89.

Finegan, Edward and Douglas Biber. 1994. "Register and social dialect variation: An integrated approach." In Douglas Biber and Edward Finegan (eds.) *Sociolinguistic Perspectives on Register,* 315–47. New York: Oxford University Press.

Fischer, John N.L. 1958. "Social influences in the choice of a linguistic variant." *Word* 14: 47–56.

Fontanella de Weinberg, Maria. 1974. *Un aspecto sociolinguistico del español bonaerense: la –s in Bahia Blanca.* Bahia Blanca: Cuadernos de Linguistica.

Fought, Carmen. 1997. "A majority sound change in a minority community:/u/-fronting in Chicano English." *Journal of Sociolinguistics* 3: 5–23.

Fought, Carmen. 2002. Ethnicity. In J.K. Chambers, Peter Trudgill, and Natalie Schilling-Estes (eds.) *The Handbook of Language Variation and Change,* 444–72. Oxford: Blackwell.

Fought, Carmen. 2003. *Chicano English in Context.* Basingstoke: Palgrave Macmillan.

Foulkes, Paul and Gerry Docherty (eds.) 1999. *Urban Voices: Variation and Change in British Accents* London: Arnold.

Fridland, Valerie. 1999. "The southern shift in Memphis, Tennessee." *Language Variation and Change* 11: 267–85.

Gal, Susan. 1979. *Language Shift: Social Determinants of Linguistic Change in Bilingual Austria.* New York: Academic Press.

Gee, James Paul. 1990. *Social Linguistics and Literacies: Ideology in Discourses.* London: Falmer.

Gee, James Paul. 1999. *An Introduction to Discourse Analysis: Theory and Method.* London: Routledge.

Gilbert, D. 2003. *The American Class Structure in an Age of Growing Inequality.* Belmont, CA: Thomson.

Giles, Howard. 1979. "Ethnicity markers in speech." In Klaus R. Scherer and Howard Giles (eds.) *Social Markers in Speech,* 251–89. Cambridge: Cambridge University Press.

Giles, Howard and Peter E. Powesland. 1975. *Speech Style and Social Evaluation.* New York: Academic Press.

Glazer, Nathan and Daniel P. Moynihan. 1963 *Beyond the Melting Pot: The Negroes, Puerto Ricans, Jews, Italians, and Irish of New York City*. Cambridge, Mass.: M.I.T. and Harvard Press.

Goffman, Erving. 1981. *Forms of Talk*. Philadelphia: University of Pennsylvania Press.

Goodwin, Charles. 1984. "Notes on story structure and the organization of participation." In J. Maxwell Atkinson and John Heritage (eds.) *Structures of Social Action: Studies in Conversational Analysis*, 225–46. Cambridge: Cambridge University Press.

Gordon, Matthew J. 2001. *Small-town Values and Big-city Vowels: A Study of the Northern Cities Shift in Michigan*. Publication of the American Dialect Society, 84. Durham, NC: Duke University Press.

Graddol, David and Joan Swann. 1989. *Gender Voices*. Oxford: Blackwell.

Gregersen, Frans and Ing Lise Pedersen (eds.) 1991. *The Copenhagen Study in Urban Sociolinguistics*, 2 vols. Copenhagen: C. A. Reitzels Forlag.

Gumperz, John. 1982. *Discourse Strategies*. Cambridge: Cambridge University Press.

Guy, Gregory, Barbara Horvath, Julia Vonwiller, Elaine Daisley, and Inge Rogers. 1986. "An intonational change in progress in Australian English." *Language in Society* 15: 23–52.

Habick, Timothy. 1980. Sound change in Farmer City: A sociolinguistic study based on acoustic data. Ph.D. dissertation, University of Illinois at Urbana-Champaign.

Haeri, Nilofaar. 1996. *The Sociolinguistic Market of Cairo: Gender, Class, and Education*. London: Kegan Paul International.

Hazen, Kirk. 2000. *Identity and Ethnicity in the Rural South: A Sociolinguistic View through Past and Present BE*. Publication of the American Dialect Society 83. Durham, NC: Duke University Press.

Hazen, Kirk. 2007. "The study of variation in historical perspective." In Robert Bayley and Ceil Lucas (eds.) *Sociolinguistic Variation: Theories, Methods, and Applications*, 70–89. Cambridge: Cambridge University Press.

Hindle, Donald. 1978. "Approaches to vowel normalization in the study of natural speech." In David Sankoff (ed.) *Linguistic Variation: Models and Methods*, 161–71. New York: Academic Press.

Hindle, Donald. 1979. The social and situational condition of phonetic variation. Unpublished PhD dissertation, University of Pennsylvania.

Holmes, Janet. 1988. "Paying compliments: A sex-preferential positive politeness strategy." *Journal of Pragmatics* 12: 445–65.

Holmes, Janet. 1990. "Apologies in New Zealand English." *Language in Society* 19: 155–99.

Holmes, Janet. 2006. *Gendered Talk at Work: Constructing Gender through Workplace Discourse*. Oxford: Blackwell.

Horvath, Barbara. M. 1985. *Variation in Australian English: The Sociolects of Sydney*. Cambridge: Cambridge University Press.

Hunston, Susan. 2002. *Corpora in Applied Linguistics*. Cambridge: Cambridge University Press.

Hymes, Dell. 1972. "Models of the interaction of language and social life." In John J. Gumperz and Dell Hymes (eds.) *Directions in Sociolinguistics: The Ethnography of Communication*, 35–71. New York: Holt, Rinehart and Winston.

Hymes, Dell. 1974. *Foundations in Sociolinguistics: An Ethnographic Approach.* Philadelphia: University of Pennsylvania Press.

Hymes, Dell. 1981. *"In vain I tried to tell you"* – *Essays in Native American Ethnopoetics.* (Studies in Native American Literature, No. 1.) Philadelphia: University of Pennsylvania Press.

Hymes, Dell. 1996. *Ethnography, Linguistics, Narrative Inequality: Toward an Understanding of Voice.* London: Taylor and Francis.

Igoe, Matthew, Nel Lamb, Jon Gilman, and Ron Kim. 1999. The further grammaticalization of *be like* and some observations on *be all*. Paper given at NWAV-28, University of Toronto, October 1999.

Iri, Masao. 1959. "A mathematical method in phonetics with a special reference to the acoustical structure of Japanese vowels." *Gengo Kenkyu* 35: 23–30.

Irvine, Judith T. 1979. "Formality and informality in speech events." *American Anthropologist* 81.773–90.

Irvine, Judith T. 1990." Registering affect: Heteroglossia in the linguistic expression of emotion." In Catherine A. Lutz and Lila Abu-Lughod (eds.) 1990. *Language and the Politics of Emotion*, 126–61. Cambridge: Cambridge University Press.

Jefferson, Gail, Harvey Sacks, and Emanuel A Schegloff. 1987. Notes on laughter in pursuit of intimacy. In Graham Button and John R.E. Lee (eds.) *Talk and Social Organisation*. Clevedon, 152–205. Avon: Multilingual Matters.

Johnstone, Barbara. 1996. *The Linguistic Individual.* New York: Oxford University Press.

Johnstone, Barbara and Judith Mattson Bean. 1997. Self-expression and linguistic variation. *Language in Society* 26: 221–46.

Jones-Sargent, Val. 1983. *Tyne Bytes: A Computerized Study of Tyneside.* Frankfurt: Peter Lang.

Joseph, John Earl. 1987. *Eloquence and Power: The Rise of Language Standards and Standard Languages.* London: Frances Pinter.

Katriel, Tamar. 1986. *Talking Straight: Dugri speech in Israeli Sabra Culture.* Cambridge: Cambridge University Press.

Keenan, Elinor. 1974. "Norm-makers, norm-breakers: Uses of speech by men and women in a Malagasay community." In Richard Bauman and Joel Sherzer (eds.) *Explorations in the Ethnography of Speaking*, 125–53. Cambridge: Cambridge University Press.

Kellas, James G. 1968. *Modern Scotland: The Nation since 1870.* New York: Praeger.

Kellas, James G. 1980. *Modern Scotland*, (2nd edn) London: Allen and Unwin.

Kerswill, Paul. 1987. "Levels of linguistic variation in Durham." *Journal of Linguistics* 23: 25–49.

Kerswill, Paul. 1996. Children, adolescents and language change. *Language Change and Variation* 8: 177–202.

Kerswill, Paul and Ann Williams. 2000. "Creating a new town koine: children and language change in Milton Keynes." *Language in Society* 29: 65–115.

Kerswill, Paul, Eivind Torgersen, and Susan Fox. 2008. "Reversing 'drift': Innovation and diffusion in the London diphthong system." *Language Variation and Change* 20.

Kerswill, Paul and Susan Wright. 1990. "On the limits of auditory transcription: a sociophonetic perspective." *Language Variation and Change* 2: 255–75.

King, Ruth. 2005. "Morphosyntactic variation and theory: Subject-verb agreement in Acadian French." In Leonie Cornips and Karen P. Corrigan (eds.) *Syntax and Variation: Reconciling the biological and the social*, 199–229. Amsterdam: John Benjamins.

Kroch, Anthony S. 1978. Toward a theory of social dialect variation. *Language in Society* 7.17–36.

Kroch, Anthony S. 1995. Dialect and style in the speech of upper class Philadelphia. In Gregory R. Guy, Crawford Feagin, Deborah Schiffrin, and John Baugh (eds.) *Towards a Social Science of Language: Papers in honor of William Labov*, vol. 1, 23–45. Amsterdam: John Benjamins.

Kytő, Merja. 1997. "*Be/have* + past participle: The choice of the auxiliary with intransitives from Late Middle English to Modern English." In Matti Rissanen, Merja Kytő, and Kirsi Heikkonen (eds.) *English in Transition: Corpus-based Studies in Linguistic Variation and Genre Style*,17–85. Berlin: Mouton de Gruyter.

Labov, William. 1963. "The social motivation of a sound change." *Word* 19: 273–309.

Labov, William. 1966. *The Social Stratification of English in New York City*. Washington, D. C.: Center for Applied Linguistics.

Labov, William. 1969. Contraction, deletion, and inherent variability of the English copula. *Language* 45: 715–62.

Labov, William. 1972a. *Sociolinguistic Patterns*. Philadelphia: University of Pennsylvania Press.

Labov, William. 1972b. *Language in the Inner City: Studies in the Black English Vernacular*. Philadelphia: University of Pennsylvania Press.

Labov, William. 1981. Field methods of the project on linguistic change and variation. *Sociolinguistic Working Paper, No. 81.* Austin: Southwest Educational Development Laboratory.

Labov, William. 1994. *Principles of Linguistic Change: Internal Factors.* Oxford: Blackwell.

Labov, William. 2001. *Principles of Linguistic Change: Social factors.* Oxford: Blackwell.

Labov, William. 2006. *The Social Stratification of English in New York City,* (2nd edn) Cambridge: Cambridge University Press.

Labov, William and Joshua Waletztky. 1967. Narrative analysis: Oral versions of personal experience. In June Helm (ed.) *Essays on the Verbal and Visual Arts*, 12–44. Seattle: University of Washington Press.

Lippi-Green, Rosina L. 1989. Social network integration and language change in progress in an alpine rural village. *Language in Society* 18: 213–34.

Labov, William, Paul Cohen, Clarence Robins, and John Lewis. 1968. *A Study of the Non-standard English of Negro and Puerto Rican Speakers in New York City.* Cooperative Research Project No. 3288. New York: Columbia University.

Labov, William, Malcah Yaeger, and Richard Steiner. 1972. *A Quantitative Study of Sound Change in Progress*. Philadelphia: U.S. Regional Survey.

Labov, William, Sharon Ash, and Charles Boberg. 2006. *The Atlas of North American English: Phonetics, Phonology and Sound Change*. Berlin: Mouton de Gruyter.

Lavendera, Beatriz R. 1978. "Where does the sociolinguistic variable stop?" *Language in Society* 7: 171–82.

Leech, Geoffrey. 1997. "Introducing corpus annotation." In Roger Garside, Geoffrey Leech, and Anthony McEnery (eds.) *Corpus Annotation: Linguistic Information from Computer Text Corpora*, 1–18. London: Longman.

Lees, Robert B. 1957. "Review of Noam Chomsky *Syntactic Structures*." *Language* 33: 375–407.

Lein, Laura and Donald Brenneis. 1978. "Children's disputes in three speech communities." *Language in Society* 7: 299–323.

Levey, Stephen. 2008. Quotative variation in later childhood: Insights from London preadolescents. Paper given at Sociolinguistics Symposium 17, Amsterdam, April.

Llamas, Carmen. 2006. "Shifting identities and orientations in a border town." In Tope Omoniyi and Goodith White (eds.) *The Sociolinguistics of Identity*, 92–112. London: Continuum.

Lofland, John, David A. Snow, Leon Anderson, and Lyn H. Lofland. 2006. *Analyzing Social Settings: A Guide to Qualitative Observation and Analysis*, (4th edn) Belmont, CA: Wadsworth/Thomson Learning.

Macafee, Caroline. 1994. *Traditional Dialect in the Modern World*. Frankfurt: Peter Lang.

Macaulay, Ronald K.S. 1970. "Review of Walt A. Wolfram: *A Sociolinguistic Description of Detroit Negro Speech*." *Language* 46: 764–73.

Macaulay, Ronald K.S. 1974. "Review of Ralph Fasold *Tense Marking in Black English*." *Language* 50: 758–62.

Macaulay, Ronald K.S. 1975. Linguistic insecurity. In J. Derrick McClure (ed.) *The Scots Language in Education,* 35–43. Aberdeen: Aberdeen College of Education. (Reprinted in Macaulay 1997.)

Macaulay, Ronald K.S. 1976a. "Review of Peter Trudgill *The Social Differentiation of English in Norwich*". *Language* 52: 226–70.

Macaulay, Ronald K.S. 1976b. "Social class and language in Glasgow." *Language in Society* 5: 173–88.

Macaulay, Ronald K.S. 1977. *Language, Social Class, and Education: A Glasgow Study*. Edinburgh: Edinburgh University Press.

Macaulay, Ronald K.S. 1978. Variation and consistency in Glaswegian English. In Peter Trudgill (ed.) *Sociolinguistic Patterns in British English*, 132–43. London: Edward Arnold.

Macaulay, Ronald K.S. 1984. "Chattering, nattering and blethering: Informal interviews as speech events." In Werner Enninger and Lilith M. Haynes (eds.) *Studies in Language Ecology,* 51–64. Wiesbaden: Franz Steiner Verlag.

Macaulay, Ronald K.S. 1985. The narrative skills of a Scottish coal miner. In Manfred Görlach (ed.) *Focus on: Scotland*, 101–24. Amsterdam: Benjamins.

Macaulay, Ronald K.S. 1987. The sociolinguistic significance of Scottish dialect humor. *International Journal of the Sociology of Language*, 65: 53–63.

Macaulay, Ronald K.S. 1988a. "The rise and fall of the vernacular." In Caroline Duncan-Rose and Theo Venneman (eds.) *On language: Rhetorica, Phonologica, Syntactica: Festschrift for Robert P. Stockwell*. London: Routledge, 106–13. [Reprinted in Macaulay 1997.]

Macaulay, Ronald K.S. 1988b. "Linguistic change and stability." In K. Ferrara, B. Brown, K. Walters, and J. Baugh (eds.) *Linguistic Change and Contact*, 225–31. Austin: University of Texas.

Macaulay, Ronald K.S. 1991a. *Locating Dialect in Discourse: The Language of Honest Men and Bonnie Lasses in Ayr*. New York: Oxford University Press.

Macaulay, Ronald K.S. 1991b. 'Coz it izny spelt when they say it': Displaying dialect in writing. *American Speech* 66: 280–91.

Macaulay, Ronald K.S. 1995. "The adverbs of authority." *English World-Wide* 16: 37–60.

Macaulay, Ronald K.S. 1997. *Standards and Variation in Urban Speech: Examples from Lowland Scots*. Amsterdam: John Benjamins.

Macaulay, Ronald K.S. 1999. "Is sociolinguistics lacking in style?" *Cuadernos de Filología Inglesa* 8: 9–33.

Macaulay, Ronald K.S. 2001a. "*You're like 'why not?'* The quotative expressions of Glasgow adolescents." *Journal of Sociolinguistics* 5. 3–21.

Macaulay, Ronald K.S. 2001b. "The question of genre." In Penelope Eckert and John R. Rickford (eds.) *Style and Sociolinguistic Variation*, 78–82. Cambridge: Cambridge University Press.

Macaulay, Ronald K.S. 2002. "Extremely interesting, very interesting, or only quite interesting? Adverbs and social class." *Journal of Sociolinguistics* 6: 398–417.

Macaulay, Ronald K.S. 2003. "Repeat after me: The value of replication." *International Journal of English Studies* 3: 77–92.

Macaulay, Ronald K.S. 2005a. *Talk that Counts: Age, Gender, and Social Class Differences in Discourse*. New York: Oxford University Press.

Macaulay, Ronald K.S. 2005b. *Extremely Common Eloquence: Constructing Scottish Identity through Narrative*. Amsterdam: Rodopi.

Macaulay, Ronald K.S. 2006a. *The Social Art: Language and Its Uses*, (2nd edn) New York: Oxford University Press.

Macaulay, Ronald K.S. 2006b. "*Pure* grammaticalization: The development of a teenage intensifier." *Language Variation and Change* 18: 267–83.

Macaulay, Ronald K.S. 2008. Adolescents and identity. Paper given at Sociolinguistics Symposium 17, Amsterdam, April.

Macaulay, Ronald K.S. and Gavin D. Trevelyan. 1973. Language, Education and Employment in Glasgow. (Final report to the Social Science Research Council) Edinburgh: The Scottish Council for Research in Education.

Maltz, Daniel N. and Ruth A. Borker. 1982. A cultural approach to male-female miscommunication. In John J. Gumperz (ed.) *Language and Social Identity*, 195–216. Cambridge: Cambridge University Press.

Manes, Joan and Nessa Wolfson. 1981. The compliment formula. In Florian Coulmas (ed.) *Conversational Routine*, 115–132. The Hague: Mouton.

Mann, V.A. 1986. "Phonological awareness: The role of reading experience." *Cognition* 24: 65–92.

Mather, James Y. and Hans-Henning Speitel. 1975–1986. *The Linguistic Atlas of Scotland: Scots Section*, 3 vols. London: Croom Helm.

Maybin, Janet. 2006. *Children's Voices*. Basingstoke: Palgrave Macmillan.

McCafferty, Kevin. 2001. *Ethnicity and Language Change: English in (London) Derry, Northern Ireland*. Amsterdam: John Benjamins.

McNair, Elizabeth DuPree. 2005. *Mill Villagers and Farmers: Dialect and Economics in a Small Southern Town*. Publication of the American Dialect Society 90. Durham, NC: Duke University Press.

Mendoza-Denton, Norma. 2002. Language and identity. In J.K. Chambers, Peter Trudgill, and Natalie Schilling-Estes (eds.) *The Handbook of Language Variation and Change*, 475–99. Oxford: Blackwell.

Mendoza-Denton, Norma, Jennifer Hay, and Stefanie Jannedy. 2003. "Probabilistic sociolinguistics beyond variable rules." In Rens Bod, Jennifer Hay, and Stefanie Jannedy (eds.), *Probabilistic Linguistics* 97–138. Cambridge, Mass.: MIT Press.

Meyerhoff, Miriam. 1996. "Dealing with gender identity as a sociolinguistic variable." In Victoria L. Bergvall, Janet M. Bing, and Alice E Freed (eds.) *Rethinking Language and Gender Research: Theory and Practice*, 202–27. London: Longman.

Meyerhoff, Miriam. 2001. "Communities of practice." In J. K. Chambers, Peter Trudgill, and Natalie Schilling-Estes (eds.) *The Handbook of Language Variation and Change*, 526–48. Oxford: Blackwell.

Milroy, James, Lesley Milroy, Sue Hartley, and David Walshaw. 1994. "Glottal stops and Tyneside glottalization: Competing patterns of variation and change." *Language Variation and Change* 4, 327–57.

Milroy, Lesley. 1980. *Language and Social Networks*. Oxford: Basil Blackwell.

Milroy, Lesley. 1987. *Language and Social Networks* (2nd edn) Oxford: Basil Blackwell.

Milroy, Lesley. 2001. The social categories of race and class: Language ideology and sociolinguistics. In Nikolas Coupland, Srikani Sarangi, and Christopher N. Candlin (eds.) *Sociolinguistics and Social Theory*, 235–60. London: Pearson Education.

Milroy, Lesley. 2002. "Social networks." In J. K. Chambers, Peter Trudgill, and Natalie Schilling-Estes (eds.) *The Handbook of Language Variation and Change*, 549–72. Oxford: Blackwell.

Milroy, Lesley. 2004. "Language ideologies and linguistic change." In Carmen Fought (ed.) *Sociolinguistic Variation: Critical Reflections*, 161–77. New York: Oxford University Press.

Milroy, Lesley and James Milroy. 1977. "Speech and context in an urban setting." *Belfast Working Papers in Language and Linguistics*, 2 (1): 1–85.

Milroy, Lesley and Matthew Gordon. 2003. *Sociolinguistics: Method and Interpretation*. Oxford: Blackwell.

Mitchell, Alexander George and Arthur Delbridge. 1965a. *The Pronunciation of English in Australia*. Sydney: Angus and Robertson.

Mitchell, Alexander George and Arthur Delbridge. 1965b. *The Speech of Australian Adolescents*. Sydney: Angus and Robertson.

Munroe, Robert L. and Ruth H. Munroe. 1991. "Comparative field studies: Methodological issues and future possibilities." *Behavior Science Research* 25: 155–85.

Nearey, Terence Michael. 1978. Phonetic feature systems for vowels. Ph.D. dissertation, University of Alberta.

Nolan, Francis and Paul Kerswill. 1990. "The description of connected speech processes." In S. Ramsaran (ed.) *Essays in Honour of A.C. Gimson*, 295–316. London: Routledge.

Nordberg, Bengt. 1969. "The urban dialect of Eskiltuna, methods and problems." In Hreinn Benediktsson (ed.) *The Nordic Languages and Modern Linguistics*, 426–43. Reykjavík: Visindafélag Íslendinga 39.

Nylvek, J.A. 1992. A sociolinguistic analysis of Canadian English in Saskatchewan: A look at urban versus rural. Unpublished PhD dissertation, University of Victoria.

O'Connell, Daniel C. and Sabine Kowal. 2008. *Communicating with One Another: toward a Psychology of Spontaneous Discourse*. New York: Springer.

Ochs, Elinor, Ruth Smith, and Carolyn Taylor. 1989. "Detective stories at dinnertime: Problem-solving through narration. *Cultural Dynamics* 2." (Reprinted in Donald Brenneis and Ronald K.S. Macaulay (eds.) *The Matrix of Language: Contemporary Linguistic Anthropology,* 39–55. Boulder, CO: Westview Press.)

Orton, Harold. 1962. *Survey of English Dialects: Introduction*. Leeds: Arnold.

Paolillo, John C. 2002. *Analyzing Linguistic Variation: Statistical Models and Methods*. Stanford, CA: CSLI Publications.

Pellowe, John, Barbara M.H. Strang, Graeme Nixon, and V. McNeany. 1972. A dynamic modeling of linguistic variation: the urban (Tyneside) linguistic survey. *Lingua* 30: 1–30.

Pittinger, Robert E., Charles F. Hockett, and John J. Danehy. 1960. *The First Five Minutes: A Sample of Microscopic Interview Analysis*. Ithaca: Martineau.

Pope, Jennifer, Miriam Meyerhoff, and D. Robert Ladd. 2007. "Forty years of language change on Martha's Vineyard." *Language* 83: 615–27.

Preston, Dennis. R. 1985. "The Li'l Abner syndrome: Written representations of speech." *American Speech* 60: 328–36.

Preston, Dennis R. 1991. "Sorting out the variables in sociolinguistic theory." *American Speech* 66: 33–56.

Preston, Dennis R. 2001. "Style and the psycholinguistics of sociolinguistics: the logical problem of language variation." In Penelope Eckert and John R. Rickford (eds.) *Style and Sociolinguistic Variation*, 279–304. Cambridge: Cambridge University Press.

Preston, Dennis. R. 2002. "Language with an attitude." In J.K. Chambers, Peter Trudgill, and Natalie Schilling-Estes (eds.) *The Handbook of Language Variation and Change*, 40–66.

Quirk, Randolph, Sidney Greenbaum, Geoffrey Leech, and Jan Svartvik. 1985. *A Comprehensive Grammar of the English Language*. London: Longman.

Rampton, Ben. 1992. Scope for empowerment in sociolinguistics? In Deborah Cameron, Elizabeth Frazer, Penelope Harvey, Ben Rampton, and Kay Richardson (eds.) *Researching Language: Issues of Power and Method*, 29–64. London: Longman.

Reah, K. 1982. "The Labovian interview: A reappraisal." *Lore and Language* 3(7): 1–13.

Reid, Ivan. 1989. *Social Class Differences in Britain.* (3rd edn) London: Fontana.

Rickford, John R. 1997. Unequal partnership: Sociolinguistics and the African American speech community. *Language in Society* 26: 161–197.

Rickford, John R. and Faye McNair-Knox. 1994. "Addressee- and topic-influenced style shift: A quantitative sociolinguistic study." In Douglas Biber and Edward Finegan (eds.) *Sociolinguistic Perspectives on Register,* 235–76. New York: Oxford University Press.

Rissanen, Matti, Merja Kytő, and Kirsi Heikkonen (eds.) 1997a. *English in Transition: Corpus-based Studies in Linguistic Variation and Genre Styles.* Berlin: Mouton de Gruyter.

Rissanen, Matti, Merja Kytő and Kirsi Heikkonen (eds.). 1997b. *Grammaticalization at Work: Studies of Long-term Developments in English.* Berlin: Mouton de Gruyter.

Romaine, Suzanne. 1975. "Linguistic Variability in the Speech of some Edinburgh Schoolchildren." Unpublished M.Litt. thesis, University of Edinburgh.

Romaine, Suzanne. 1980. A critical overview of the methodology of urban British sociolinguistics. *English World-Wide* 1: 163–98.

Romaine, Suzanne. 1984. *The Language of Children and Adolescents: The Acquisition of Communicative Competence.* Oxford: Blackwell.

Romaine, Suzanne. 1989. "Review of Joseph 1987." *Linguistics* 27: 574–79.

Romaine. Suzanne and Deborah Lange. 1991. "The use of *like* as a marker of reported speech and thought: A case of grammaticalization in progress." *American Speech* 66: 227–79.

Rosaldo, Michelle. 1973. "I have nothing to hide: The language of Ilongot oratory." *Language in Society* 11:193–223.

Sacks, Harvey. 1992. *Lectures on Conversation* (ed. Gail Jefferson). 2 vols. Oxford: Blackwell.

Sacks, Harvey, Emanuel Schegloff, and Gail Jefferson. 1974. "A simplest systematics for the organization of turn-taking in conversation." *Language* 50: 696–735.

Sanchez, Tara and Anne Charity. 1999. The use of *be like* and other verbs of quotation in a predominantly African-American community. Paper given at NWAV-28, University of Toronto, October 1999.

Sankoff, David. 1988. "Problems of representativeness." In Ulrich Ammon, Norbert Dittmar and Klaus J. Mattheier (eds.) *Sociolinguistics: An International Handbook of the Science of Language and Society,* 984–7. Berlin: De Gruyter.

Sankoff, Gillian. 2004. Adolescents, young adults, and the critical period: Two case studies from "Seven Up." In Carmen Fought (ed.) *Sociolinguistic Variation: Critical Reflections,* 121–39. New York: Oxford University Press.

Schiffrin, Deborah. 1987. *Discourse Markers.* Cambridge: Cambridge University Press.

Schilling-Estes, Natalie. 1998. Situated ethnicities: Constructing and reconstructing identity in the sociolinguistic interview. Paper presented at NWAV-27, University of Georgia, October.

Schilling-Estes, Natalie. 2004. "Exploring intertextuality in the sociolinguistic interview." In Carmen Fought (ed.) *Sociolinguistic Variation: Critical Reflections,* 44–61. New York: Oxford University Press.

Schneider, Edgar W. 2002. "Investigating variation and change in written documents." In J.K. Chambers, Peter Trudgill, and Natalie Schilling-Estes (eds.) *The Handbook of Language Variation and Change*, 67–96. Oxford: Blackwell.

Shuy, Roger, Walt A. Wolfram, and William K. Riley. 1968a. *Field Techniques in an Urban Language Study.* Washington, DC: Center for Applied Linguistics.

Shuy, Roger, Walt A. Wolfram, and William K. Riley. 1968b. *A Study of Social Dialects in Detroit.* Final Report to U.S. Office of Education.

Sinclair, John M. 1991. "The automatic analysis of corpora." In Jan Svartvik (ed.) *Directions in Corpus Linguistics,* 379–97. Berlin: Mouton de Gruyter.

Singler, John V. 2001. "Why you can't do a VARBRUL study of quotatives and what such a study can show us." *University of Pennsylvania Working Papers in Linguistics* 7: 257–78.

Smith, Jennifer. 2001. Negative concord in the Old and the New World: Evidence from Scotland. *Language Variation and Change* 13: 109–34.

Stenström, Anna-Brita, Gisle Andersen, and Ingrid Kristine Hasund. 2002. *Trends in Teenage Talk: Corpus Compilation, Analysis and Findings.* Amsterdam: John Benjamins.

Stuart-Smith, Jane. 1999. Glasgow. In Paul Foulkes and Gerard J. Docherty (eds.) *Urban Voices: Variation and Change in British Accents*, 203–22 London: Arnold.

Stuart-Smith, Jane. 2003. The phonology of modern Urban Scots. In John Corbett, Derrick M. McClure, and Jane Stuart-Smith (eds.) *The Edinburgh Companion to Scots*, 110–37. Edinburgh: Edinburgh University Press.

Stuart-Smith, Jane, Claire Timmins, and Fiona Tweedie. 2007. Talkin' Jockney? Variation and change in Glaswegian accent. *Journal of Sociolinguistics* 11: 221–60.

Svartvik, Jan. 1980. *Well* in conversation. In Sidney Greenbaum, Geoffrey Leech, and Jan Svartvik (eds.) *Studies in English Linguistics for Randolph Quirk,* 167–77. London: Longman.

Svartvik, Jan. 1992. Corpus linguistics comes of age. In Jan Svartvik (ed.) *Directions in Corpus Linguistics,* 7–13. Berlin: Mouton de Gruyter.

Syrdal, Ann K. and H.S. Gopal. 1986. A perceptual model of vowel recognition based on the auditory representation of American English vowels. *Journal of the Acoustical Society of America* 79: 1086–100.

Tagliamonte, Sali A. (1998) *Was/were* across the generations: View from the city of York. *Language Variation and Change* 10: 153–92.

Tagliamonte, Sali A. and Rachel Hudson. 1999. "*Be like* et al. beyond America: The quotative system in British and Canadian youth." *Journal of Linguistics* 3: 147–72.

Tagliamonte, Sali. 2006. *Analysing Sociolinguistic Variation.* Cambridge: Cambridge University Press.

Tagliamonte, Sali A. 2007. Quantitative analysis. In Robert Bayley and Ceil Lucas (eds.) *Sociolinguistic Variation: Theories, Methods, and Applications*, 70–89. Cambridge: Cambridge University Press.

Tagliamonte Sali A. and Alex D'Arcy. 2004b. Mom *said*, and my daughter's *like*: Tracking the quotative system through the generations. Paper given at NWAV-33, University of Michigan.

Tagliamonte Sali A. and Alex D'Arcy. 2004a. *"He's like, she's like*: The quotative system in Canadian youth." *Journal of Sociolinguistics* 8: 493–514.

Tannen, Deborah. 1990. *You Just Don't Understand: Women and Men in Conversation*. New York: Ballantine.

Tedlock, Dennis. 1978. *Finding the Center*. Lincoln, NB: University of Nebraska Press.

Tedlock, Dennis. 1983. *The Spoken Word and the Work of Interpretation*. Philadelphia: University of Pennsylvania Press.

Thakerar, Jitendra N., Howard Giles and Jenny Cheshire. 1982. "Psychological and linguistic parameters of speech accommodation theory." In Colin Fraser and Klaus R. Scherer (eds.) *Advances in the Social Psychology of Language*, 205–55. Cambridge: Cambridge University Press.

Thomas, Erik R. 2002. "Instrumental phonetics." In J. K. Chambers, Peter Trudgill, and Natalie Schilling-Estes (eds.) *The Handbook of Language Variation and Change*, 168–200. Oxford: Blackwell.

Traugott, Elizabeth and Suzannne Romaine. 1985. "Some questions for the definition of 'Style' in sociohistorical linguistics." *Folia Linguistica* 6:7–39.

Trudgill, Peter. 1974. *The Social Differentiation of English in Norwich*. Cambridge: Cambridge University Press.

Vaughn-Cooke, A. Fay. 2007. "Lessons learned from the Ebonics controversy: implications for language assessment." In Robert Bayley and Ceil Lucas (eds.) *Sociolinguistic Variation: Theories, Methods, and Applications*, 254–75. Cambridge: Cambridge University Press.

Vihmann, Marilyn May. 1996. *Phonological Development: The Origins of Language in the Child*. Oxford: Blackwell.

Vuchinich, Samuel. 1990. "The sequential organization of closing in verbal family conflict." In Allen D. Grimshaw (ed.) *Conflict Talk: Sociolinguistic Investigations of Arguments in Conversations,* 118–38. Cambridge: Cambridge University Press.

Warner, W.L., M. Meeker and K. Eeels (1949) *Social Class in America*. Chicago: Science Research Associates.

Watt, Dominic and Lesley Milroy. 1999. "Patterns of variation and change in three Newcastle vowels: Is this dialect leveling?" In Paul Foulkes and Gerry Docherty (eds.) *Urban Voices: Variation and Change in British Accents,* 25–46. London: Arnold.

Wilson, Sir James. 1923. *The Dialect of Robert Burns as Spoken in Central Ayrshire*. Oxford: Oxford University Press.

Wodak, Ruth. 2006. "Dilemmas of discourse." *Language in Society* 35: 595–611.

Wolfram, Walt. 1969. *A Sociolinguistic Description of Detroit Negro speech*. Washington, DC: Center for Applied Linguistics.

Wolfram, Walt. 1973. *Sociolinguistic Aspects of Assimilation: Puerto Rican English in New York City*. Arlington: Center for Applied Linguistics.

Wolfram, Walt. 1993. Identifying and interpreting variables. In Dennis Preston (ed.) *American Dialect Research*, 193–221. Amsterdam: John Benjamins.

Wolfram, Walt and Clare J. Dannenberg. 1999. "Dialect identity in a tri-ethnic context: The case of Lumbee American Indian English." *English World-Wide* 20: 179–216.

Wolfram, Walt and Erik R. Thomas. 2002. *The Development of African American English*. Oxford: Blackwell.

Wolfson, Nessa. 1976. "Speech events and natural speech: Some implications for sociolinguistic methodology." *Language in Society*: 189–209.

Wolfson, Nessa. 1978. A feature of performed narrative: The conversational historical present. *Language in Society* 7: 215–39.

Zwicky, Arnold M. 1972. "Note on a phonological hierarchy in English." In Robert P. Stockwell and Ronald K.S. Macaulay (eds.) *Linguistic change and generative theory*, 275–301. Bloomington: Indiana University Press.

Name Index

Aijmer, K. 27
Altenberg, B. 27
Andersen, G. 5, 33, 34, 78–80
Argyle, M. 10, 15
Ash, S. 39
Azoulay, K.G. 9

Bailey, G. x, xi, xii, 1, 4, 7, 32
Bakhtin, M.M. 46, 49
Barth, F. 8
Bauman, R. 50
Bayley, R. 54, 55, 56
Bean, J.M. 51, 52
Bell, A. xi, 32, 45, 46, 48–9, 50, 52
Bell, B. 98
Berdan, R.H. 29, 41, 53, 54
Bernstein, B. 27, 106
Biber, D. 30, 94
Blake, R. 104
Blyth, C., Jr. 98
Boberg, C. 39
Borker, R.A. 7
Bortoni-Ricardo, S.M. 16
Bourdieu, P. 50
Brenneis, D. 89
Bright, W. vii, viii
Bucholz, M. 20
Buchstaller, I. 98

Cameron, D. 7
Campbell, D.T. 96
Cedergren, Henrietta 55
Chafe, W. 19, 20
Chambers, J.K. 2, 14, 39, 44
Charity, A. 98
Cheshire, J. vii, 5, 6, 7, 10, 26, 28, 35, 37, 48, 67, 68–70
Chomsky, N. viii
Cichoki, W. 29, 53, 54
Coates, J. 8, 38

Cohen, P. 60–3, 68
Conrad, S. 94
Coombs, C.H. ix, 18
Cornips, L. 4
Coupland, J. 5, 31
Coupland, N. x, xii, 5, 6, 10, 38, 48, 73
Crouch, I. 31
Cukor-Avila, P. 7, 98
Cumming, S. 119

Dailey-O'Cain, J. 44, 98
Daisley, E. 4
Danehy, J.J. 19
Dannenberg, C.J. 4, 9
D'Arcy, A. 28, 98, 99
Delbridge, A. 70
Dines, E.R. 102
Docherty, G.J. 4, 34, 42, 43, 80, 83
Dougherty, K.A. 98
Douglas-Cowie, E. xi, 34, 48
Dressler, R.A. 20
Dubois, B.L. 31
DuBois, J.W. 119
Dubois, S. 4, 16

Eckert, P. xi, 2, 5, 6, 7, 9, 12, 16, 35, 42, 52, 67, 68, 75–6
Edwards, W.F. 16
Eeels, K. 10
Eggins, S. 88
Elliott, N. 39

Fabb, N. 20
Fasold, R.W. vii, 2, 4, 6, 10, 53
Feagin, C. 2, 4, 6, 10, 35, 50, 66–7
Ferrara, K. 98
Finegan, E. 30, 94
Fischer, J.N.L. 6, 10
Fontanella de Weinberg, M. 15

131

132 NAME INDEX

Subject Index